MASERS AND LASERS

MASERS

BY

AND *LASERS*

H. ARTHUR KLEIN

HELEN HALE, *Editorial Consultant*

FRANK ALOISE, *Illustrator*

J. B. LIPPINCOTT COMPANY
PHILADELPHIA AND NEW YORK

To my children,
Laura and David

ACKNOWLEDGMENTS

AUTHORSHIP brings its austerities and agonies; but also its amenities. Among the latter one of the most pleasant is the terminal "thank you" for aid, information, and encouragement received from various people in various places. This author's thanks go out to the following:

In Britain: J. M. Burch, Light Division, National Physical Laboratories, Teddington; A. J. Allnutt and K. M. Greenland, Physics & Optics Department, British Scientific Instrument Research Association, Chislehurst, Kent; G. H. Cook, Rank Taylor Hobson, Leicester; P. E. Trier and J. C. Walling, Mullard Research Laboratories, Redhill, Surrey; G. Bontoft, Central Library, Ministry of Aviation, London.

In the U.S.A.: I. H. Braun, Film Associates of California; G. G. Barker, Raytheon Co., Lexington, Mass.; J. H. Beardsley, Perkin-Elmer Corp., Norwalk, Conn.; Guido Münch, Mount Wilson and Palomar Observatories, Carnegie Institution, California Institute of Technology, Pasadena; Edward Reese, Librarian, Hughes Research Laboratories, Malibu, Calif.; Cyril Solomons, Research Laboratory, Minneapolis Honeywell Co., Minneapolis, Minn.; Robert Vosper, Librarian of UCLA, as representative of the many staff members, especially in the Physics and Engineering-Mathematics libraries, whose kindness and courtesy were exemplary; the Bookmobile of the Los Angeles County Library system, and its librarian, Scott Paxton.

Also: Helen Hale, editorial consultant for this series of books; Ann

K. Beneduce of J. B. Lippincott Co., who smoothed stretches of the way that might otherwise have been rough; and M. C. Klein, who fortunately understands the author far better than masers or lasers.

The size of this type is no index to the magnitude of gratitude. . .

—H. ARTHUR KLEIN
Malibu, California

CONTENTS

MASERS AND LASERS

1

SOMETHING NEW HAS BEEN ADDED

A GREAT technical race is under way.

It is the race to develop the amazing new scientific devices called "masers" and "lasers."

Hundreds of physicists, engineers, and technicians are working in laboratories throughout the United States, Britain, the Soviet Union, and other technically advanced lands. Each month brings word of new and significant advances. Problems and difficulties are many, but the achievements already are impressive—and the promise for the future is enormous.

Within ten or twelve years the commercial output of maser and laser devices may well reach the value of a billion dollars annually in the United States alone. The impact of masers during their first years has been compared with that of transistors, born about a dozen years earlier. Even more attention is now focused on masers and lasers than was given to the transistor family at a similar point in its history.

13

Masers and lasers are in their infancy, all experts agree. Results so far achieved represent only a small beginning. The devices thus far operated, despite their successes, will someday seem as crude and primitive as does the Wright brothers' plane which first carried man in motor-driven flight at Kitty Hawk.

Yet even these early instruments have done what would have been impossible only a few years earlier. Here are a few of their achievements. They have—

——Served as clocks so accurate that they would not gain or lose more than one second in a thousand years. This makes possible a number of basic experiments which should vastly extend the understanding of our universe.

——Amplified microwave signals from satellites—signals so faint that they would have been lost by any other receiving equipment. Also amplified radio waves received from distant stars and nebulae, and in so doing provided the new science of radioastronomy with one of its most sensitive tools.

——Shot out beams of light so powerful, parallel, and pure that they could be concentrated into tiny points of intense energy. Result: holes "drilled" in diamonds and steel sheets by flashes briefer than one-thousandth of a second, during which temperatures generated equaled 18,000° Fahrenheit —nearly double the temperature of the sun's surface.

——Projected a beam of concentrated red light all the way to the moon, with so little spread of the beam that the "echo" or reflection was picked up again on earth after the expected number of seconds.

These are only some of the more spectacular events. Th
that are less dramatic at first sight are no less amazing wh
step by step, we learn the principles of masers and lasers. T..
is the road we shall take, starting with the near, known, and
familiar, and building to the new, strange, and amazing.

Masers and lasers provide the first positive method for generating controlled and uniform light, and lightlike radiations
which men cannot see with their eyes but can receive with
their instruments.

The name *maser* itself provides good clues to follow. It is
one of the words known as "acronyms"—each letter stands
for a word in a significant phrase: "*M*icrowave *A*mplification
by *S*timulated *E*mission of *R*adiation" = M-A-S-E-R.

Laser has the same origin, but replaces the *M* for *microwave*
with an *L* for *light*. (You use other acronyms constantly. What
do you know, for example, about the basis for the word *radar?*)

Maser and laser started only as name words (nouns), but
they are widely used today also as action words (verbs). For
example, you may hear a scientist report this way:

"Our new crystal *masered* when pump energy reached . . ."
etc. Or another may write:

"*Lasering* was observed intermittently . . ." etc.

Sometimes one encounters a shorter form—*to maze*. But
this seems not so likely to become a part of the technical language of our times as the longer verb *to maser*. *Maser* is pro-
nounced as if it were spelled *mazer*.

Now, following the clue of the final letter (r = radiation),
we shall see what makes masers and lasers amazing.

2

RADIATION—LIGHT

MICROWAVES and light are forms of radiation.

Light is the form of radiation we perceive most clearly, thanks to those superb sensors, our eyes. Naturally, light was the first form of radiation that moved men to wonder and worship. Light shines through almost every creation story told by the great religions of the world.

Thus the Bible, in its first chapter, Genesis, opens with a vision of the first beginning when all was formless, void, and dark, until the Creator decreed, "Let there be light."

Light comes to our eyes from far and near. It reaches us from the sun 93 million miles distant, and from other stars millions and multimillions of times more distant than the sun. Such light has crossed vast, almost empty spaces.

Light comes to us too from a lamp short inches away. It seems able with little change to travel through some solid objects, such as a plate-glass window, and with some important changes through other transparent objects, such as lenses or prisms.

Light is constantly "going places." It is ever on the move, from and to. Light from a lamp flashes out, instantly it seems, to be seen by an observer who may be miles away.

The velocity of light. Long ago men began to wonder: How fast does light move? Only experiment could answer positively, and for long centuries experiment was rare. Men who had time for such questions were in the habit of looking for an answer in the writings of some long-dead authority, such as Aristotle, or in sacred scriptures.

The great Galileo in Italy, a pioneer of experimental science, tried to measure the speed, or velocity of light. The methods he was able to use were crude, and seemed to support the widespread notion that light took no time at all to move from place to place—that it was instantaneous.

Later, observations by a Danish astronomer, Ole Roemer, showed strange shifts in the times when the moons of Jupiter were hidden (eclipsed) behind that giant planet. Roemer showed these shifts must be caused by the changing distances that the light had to travel in reaching his telescopes on the earth.

Light, then, did have a measurable velocity.

It has been measured quite exactly. In empty space its velocity is very nearly 186,000 miles each second. Scientists everywhere use the metric system, and this book will use it too. In metric units the velocity of light is very nearly

29,978,000,000 centimeters per second (cm. per sec.)

or 299,780,000 meters per second (m. per sec.)

or 299,780 kilometers per second (km. per sec.)

For their common calculations scientists use a convenient

"round number" for the velocity of light in centimeters per second: 3×10^{10} cm/sec.

This is simply a short, handy way to write 3 followed by 10 zeros, which means 3 times 10,000 million. The small number 10 after and above the large number 10 is called a "power sign" and tells us how many times the number below should be multiplied by itself. We see that $10^1 = 10$, $10^2 = 100$, $10^3 = 1000$, and so on.

This book will use this convenient way to write and work with very large numbers.

The velocity of light in empty space—3×10^{10} cm/sec.—is always and everywhere the same. It is what scientists call a "constant," and it is one of the basic constants of all science. Usually it is represented simply by the letter c.

Does that c look familiar? It appears again and again in the basic formulas and quantity relationships of physics. For example, it provides the key to Einstein's historic answer to the question: What equivalence, if any, exists between mass (m) of matter and the energy (E) associated with that matter?

His answer was the simple formula: $E = mc.^2$ In words this might be stated: *"the amount of energy* is equivalent to *the amount of mass* times *the velocity of light* times *the velocity of light."* (When mass is measured in grams, energy in a small unit called ergs, and the velocity of light is expressed in centimeters per second.)

Now c, we have seen, is a very large number. Hence c times c must be enormous. To write it out in full we would need a 9 followed by 20 zeroes. In our shorthand we can state it simply as 9×10^{20}.

Einstein's equivalence statement ($E = mc^2$) accordingly shows that a vast amount of energy is equivalent to a tiny

18

amount of matter, or (the same thing reversed) a tiny amount of matter is equivalent to a vast amount of energy.

The fantastic energy unlocked by nuclear devices, whether bombs for destruction or reactors for peaceful purposes, is associated with the "disappearance" of a tiny amount of mass. Similarly, a particle which gains much energy by being accelerated to a high speed behaves as if it had gained mass to a corresponding extent.

The velocity of light, c, is not a faraway concept of theoretical science. It is a practical measure, used by engineers every day. When maser light was "bounced" off the moon, scientists knew just how many seconds should elapse before they received the echo on earth. When a radar receiver indicates that an approaching aircraft is 9.3 miles distant, this figure is based quite exactly on the velocity of light (which is the same as that of the radar waves). In this case, the time required for the round trip of the radar pulse from transmitter to plane and back again to receiver would be almost exactly 0.0001 seconds (one ten thousandth of a second)!

Astronomers know that the sun's light travels about eight minutes to reach the earth, and that light from even relatively "near" stars has been on its way for years. A common unit for measuring cosmic distances is, in fact, *the light-year*—the distance traveled by light in a year.

Light is a Mixture of Colors. Men long watched in fear or delight as rainbows spread their multicolored arches in the sky. The color sequence was always the same: red, orange, yellow, green, blue, violet. (You can remember the order with the help of an aid such as the phrase, "*Roar Out, You Good Big Voice!*")

That color sequence was well established when, in the sev-

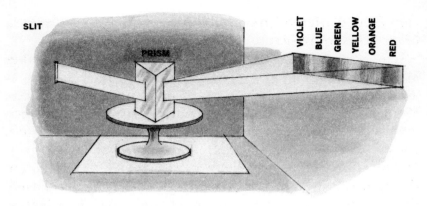

Figure 2.1 The spectrum shows that "white" light is a mixture of lights. Note that red is bent least by the prism, violet most.

enteenth century, Sir Isaac Newton brought the rainbow indoors. A giant among theorists and mathematicians, Newton was also a resourceful experimenter with a deep interest in light and optics.

Here (Figure 2.1) we see in simplified form how Newton used a glass wedge or prism to spread beams of "pure white" sunlight into a separation or spectrum of different colors, blending smoothly one into the other.

Clearly, light from a glowing body such as the sun was not one single uniform thing, but a mixture. To speak in an exact or scientific way about light, one had to specify just which part or parts of the mixture were meant, and how strong each part is compared with the others.

Newton concluded that there is no single *light,* as such. There are many *lights,* identical in velocity as they travel, but differing in other respects. These differences our eyes perceive as colors.

Today this seems obvious. But it was not always obvious. For example, a famous German poet and novelist, J. W. von Goethe, who aspired to shine also as a scientist, argued eloquently that light itself was uniform. The colors, he insisted, resulted from something that the prism had added to this pure, homogeneous light.

Facts, however, are stubborn. They continued to pile up in support of the opposite idea. But what *was* light? And what were the differences we see as colors?

The nature of light. Newton himself argued that light must be composed of streams of tiny particles or corpuscles. These flew in straight lines. Reflection occurred when they bounced from a smooth surface. Refraction took place when they were bent, as by a prism or lens. The prism sorted out the red corpuscles from the orange, those from the yellow, and so on.

Newton's particle theory of light will seem familiar and prophetic when we come to light "photons" a little later. However a whole series of important experiments showed that light behaved like no particles ever seen or dreamed of on earth.

By the early nineteenth century, in fact, most scientists were firmly convinced that light was a form of wave motion. During nearly a century this view reigned supreme. It has not been "overthrown" even now, but its rule has been greatly limited, as we shall see.

Figure 2.2 is a sketch of an experiment by Thomas Young in 1801, one of a number which seemed to establish the wave interpretation.

A lamp (L) is set up to emit light of one color only. A small beam of this light is selected by a slit in a screen (M). This travels on to another screen (N) pierced by two slits (S_1 and S_2)

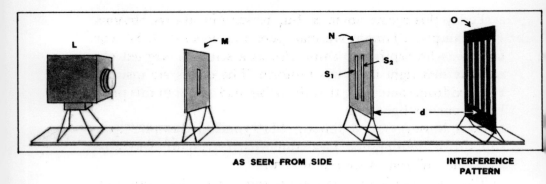

AS SEEN FROM SIDE

INTERFERENCE PATTERN

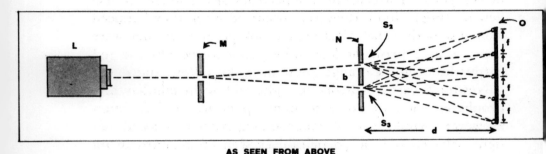

AS SEEN FROM ABOVE

Figures 2.2 and 2.3 Interference effects, such as in Young's experiment (above), established the wave theory of light at the beginning of the nineteenth century. The dotted lines in Figure 2.3 show paths of the interfering beams which produce the pattern of alternate bands of light and dark on the screen.

closely spaced. A final screen (O) receives the result.

What is it that we see on this screen?

Not two lines of light, one for each S slit, but a pattern of alternating light and dark streaks or "fringes." The brightest one is at the center, halfway between the lines of light we had *expected* would be cast by the two S slits. The others appear at regular distances to the left and right of the central fringe.

Such bands of light and dark may be produced in many other ways, if one is careful to take only a single beam of light and make it interact with itself. This interaction is called "interference."

By interference, light plus itself may be made to produce no light (the dark bands) or extra light (the light bands). How could corpuscles plus corpuscles appear as no corpuscles? Newton's particles or corpuscles, it seemed, could not account for light interference and other similar effects.

Yet wave motion constantly showed interference effects. This was true of waves on the surface of water. It was shown to be true also of the far different waves which transmit sounds through the air, and also through liquids and solids.

By means of interference experiments such as that of Young, scientists found they could measure the lengths of the waves of light of various colors. For example, if the distance between the slits on screen N is b, and the distance from screen N to screen O is d, and the separation between one fringe and the next is f, then the wave length (w) of the light emitted by the lamp is represented by this formula:

$$w = \frac{f \times b}{d}$$

Such experiments and calculations show that, for light, w is always a very small distance. For light in the midst of the red sector of the spectrum the wave length is about 0.000071 cm. (71 millionths of a centimeter). It becomes still smaller as as we move toward the violet end. In the heart of the violet zone, it is about 41 millionths of a centimeter.

We can here mention only a few of the waves of many kinds that move in the world around us. You can make waves travel

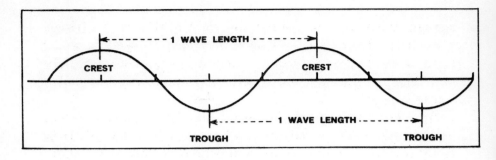

Figure 2.4 Measuring wave length. A wave length is a full wave or cycle.

along a rope by shaking one end up and down. You can make different kinds of waves "stand" on guitar strings by plucking them, or violin strings by bowing them, or piano strings by striking them.

All wave motion shares several essentials:

(1) Waves are energy changes.

(2) These changes move through the body or structure in which the waves are formed. (When the wind sends waves across a field of standing grain, it is the grain's motion which travels, not the grain itself, which remains rooted as before.)

(3) At intervals the wave pattern repeats itself. Thus waves on water alternate between crests and troughs and crests again (Figure 2.4). The distance between two corresponding points in the wave pattern is called a "wave length." Thus, crest to next crest or trough to next trough are wave-length measures.

(4) The number of full waves that move past a point in a unit of time is called the "frequency." A full wave is a cycle. Frequency is usually measured in cycles per second which we shall abbreviate as *cps*. Some waves may have to be measured in time intervals of minutes, hours, days, or longer, but those

24

we deal with here are best measured in intervals of seconds.

(5) Wave motion is described by three basic measures—wave length (w), frequency (f), and velocity (v) with which the wave travels in the direction of its motion.

A simple and convenient relation permits us to learn any of these measures if we know the other two. Frequency times wave length equals velocity ($f \times w = v$). Then frequency must equal velocity divided by wave length ($f = \frac{v}{w}$) and wave length must equal velocity divided by frequency ($w = \frac{v}{f}$).

These relationships are true for light and all other forms of radiation. They are used also in study of the wave motions we call sound.

It is easy to calculate that red light with a wave length of 71 millionths of a centimeter must oscillate with a frequency of about 424 million million times per second! Its frequency, set down in the scientific way, is 4.24×10^{14} cps.

These enormous frequencies increase as we move upward from the red toward the violet end of the spectrum. Here (Figure 2.5) are some frequencies midway in the principal color zones. All are in the 10^{14} cps range: Red 4.23. Orange 4.83. Yellow 5.25. Green 5.76. Blue 6.39. Violet 7.32.

We find, further, that the visible extremes of the spectrum are at about 3.94×10^{14} for the "lowest" visible red, and 7.7×10^{14} cps for the "highest" visible violet.

Dogs can hear sound frequencies higher than can man. Some insects, such as bees, appear able to *see* or respond to light frequencies higher than the 7.7 point. They see what we call *ultra*violet light.

Frequency, measured in cps, will appear many times in the following pages. It is a helpful way to measure radiation. Wave length shrinks when light travels through a transparent

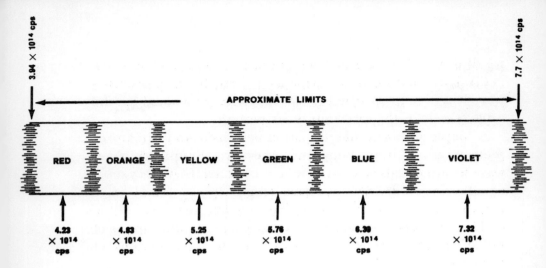

Figure 2.5 Typical frequencies of the midpoints of colors composing "white" light.

(All stated in cycles per second—cps)
(10^{14} cps equals 100,000,000,000,000 cps)

solid such as glass or diamond. The more "refractive" such a substance is, the more it slows the light which passes through it. Slowing the light means reducing its wave length. However, the frequency does not alter. It is independent of the medium through which the light passes.

Also, as we shall see shortly, the frequency of light and the way it transmits energy are very closely related, related in a way which helped scientists to discover the principles on which masers and lasers are based.

When scientists measure light wave lengths, as they often do, they commonly use either a unit called the *micron*, one millionth of a meter (or 10^{-6} m.) long, or one known as the angstrom (Å), only one 100-millionth cm. (or 10^{-8} cm.) long. This unit, named in honor of a Scandinavian student of light, is commonly used in spectroscopy—the detailed study of the spectrum of light, both visible and invisible. So precise has spectroscopy become that it sometimes uses decimals at the end of wave-length measures, such as 3978.2 Å.

In terms of angstrom units it is convenient to recall that the full range of visible light is less than 4000 Å wide, from 3900 Å for the shortest visible violet to 7600 Å for the longest visible red. The average width of each of the six principal color zones of the spectrum of white light is a little over 600 Å. Here (Figure 2.6) is the visible spectrum marked in angstroms.

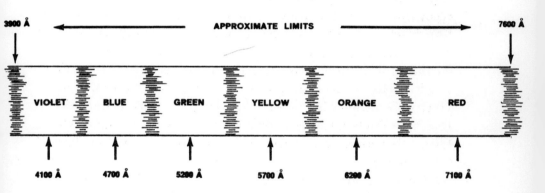

Figure 2.6 Typical wave lengths of the midpoints of colors composing "white" light.

(All stated in angstroms—Å)
(1 angstrom equals 0.00000001 cm. or 10^{-8} cm.)

Note that the wave-length scale tends to compress distances at the violet and lengthen those at the red end, while the frequency scale, shown in Figure 2.5, has the opposite effect.

Note that a wave-length display, such as this, increases from violet toward red; but a frequency display, such as Figure 2.5, increases from red toward violet. Wave length and frequency are **inversely** proportional to each other.

27

Remember this about the spectrum: Though the highest violet has a frequency less than double that of the lowest red, there is an enormous cps difference between the two. This frequency gap, in fact, is 3.7×10^{14} cps.

This means that the top, or violet color results from vibrations which take place 370 million million times more frequently each second than the vibrations which result in the bottom, or red color.

This difference—370,000,000,000,000 cps—represents a vast band width. The idea of band width means much to engineers who work with human communications, as we shall see. Such communications include both transmission and storage (or recording) of information of many kinds. Some communication reaches our ears as speech, song, music. Some reaches our eyes as pictures, either still or moving. Some is contained in meaningful numbers, codes, and data patterns of many kinds.

Think for a moment about recording and transmission of voice and music. How wide is the frequency band here? Very fine hi-fi (high fidelity) is provided by a set or system which faithfully reproduces tones all the way from a pitch as low as 20 cps to one as high as 50,000 cps. For extra good measure, let us demand a range nearly twice as broad—100,000 cps. This seems a broad band width by the standards of human ears.

Yet the band width of the spectrum of visible light is 10 million times as wide!

Clearly the vibrations of even the "lowest" visible light are extremely rapid compared with the actions and reactions of human minds and nerves. We can think of it this way, too: The pattern, or "grain," of the process we call light is extremely fine compared with the pattern or grain of our hearing, seeing, and understanding processes.

Now, we know that to write a very tiny message or make a very detailed drawing we need paper that is uniform in texture and fine-grained. A sheet that is coarse-grained, irregular, and spotty will not do. Could uniform light of a single, steady color serve as a sort of fine-grained medium for carrying the messages of voice, music, pictures, and other human information?

We shall see in this step-by-step story that it can do just that. Thanks to the amazing accomplishments of the new maser and laser "machines," light itself is about to be added to man's carriers of communications, with possibilities more far-reaching than we can now imagine.

To learn how and why, we shall now follow paths that lead through related areas: magnetism and electrification. We shall linger a little in the scientific region known as "electromagnetic vibrations." Relatively it is a new-found land, for it was unknown to Newton and even to Faraday. Yet even there we shall not halt, for beyond lies another world of physical concepts that are newer and stranger still—the world of the quantum.

3

RADIATION—BEYOND LIGHT

THE MOTIONS of water particles at or near the surface form the ripples and waves that spread over the surface of water. . . .

The waves of compression and its opposite, rarefaction, spreading through air form sound waves. . . .

But when light oscillates trillions of times per second, just *what* is oscillating?

Such questions were long puzzling. The best answer was based on ideas drawn from other parts of the swiftly growing field of physics—from the study of electrical and magnetic effects.

The scientific study of radiation problems has often shown seeming detours. Theoretical studies of magnetism, electricity, heat and temperature, structure of matter, etc., have brought new understanding of radiation.

During the first half of the nineteenth century, many basic discoveries were made in electricity and magnetism. A notable leader in this was Michael Faraday. He lacked mathematical skills but was a brilliant experimenter, a faithful follower of facts, and had a fine imagination.

To explain his findings he developed the idea of the "field" of force. Every magnet can be represented by a system of "lines of force" which, by their directions, show how other magnetic bodies, if near enough, will be attracted or repelled. In Figure

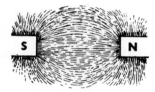

Figure 3.1 Lines of force, showing how unlike poles attract each other.

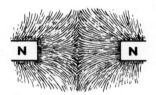

Figure 3.2 Lines of force, showing how like poles repel each other.

3.1 we see how one "north pole" attracts a "south pole"; while Figure 3.2 shows the force lines formed when one "north pole" repels another.

Similarly we can visualize lines of electrical force around charged bodies. They show how bodies of unlike charge attract each other, and how bodies of like charge repel each other.

So far, the magnetic and electrical fields appear separate. The great discoveries on which modern electrical technology is based were these:

(1) A change in strength or position of the lines of force of a magnetic field exerts force on electrically charged bodies within that field. In other words, magnetic-field changes have electrical-field results.

31

(2) The reverse of the foregoing—A change in strength or position of an electrical field exerts force on magnetic bodies within that field. In other words, electrical-field changes have magnetic-field results.

Thus an electric current through a wire deflects a magnet placed near it (the current consisting of a flow of negative electric charges commonly called "electrons"). On the other hand, moving the magnet near the wire induces a flow of electrons in that wire.

Electrical and magnetic fields obviously were parts of a single field system.

It was James Clark Maxwell, a brilliant theorist and mathematician, who first—about 100 years ago—developed the equations to show what must happen in the "electromagnetic field" created by a moving electrified particle.

Maxwell found that the resulting field changes must be radiated outward from any such moving or oscillating particle. These field changes would appear as vibrations at right angles to the direction of the wave motion. The electrical-field changes would lie at right angles also to the magnetic-field changes.

The picture was like that shown here (Figure 3.3).

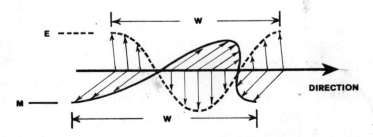

Figure 3.3 Scheme of a single electromagnetic wave. M is pattern of variation of magnetic force. E is pattern of variation of electrical force, at right angles to the magnetic. W is one wave length.

Maxwell found, further, a remarkable fact. The velocity with which these waves must travel outward was *very* close to the velocity of light as it had been measured by Fizeau, a French experimenter. It seemed entirely too close to be a mere coincidence.

Maxwell concluded, in fact, that "we can scarcely avoid the inference that light consists in the transverse undulations of the same medium which is the cause of electric and magnetic phenomena."

That medium Maxwell called "the electromagnetic field" because "it has to do with space in the neighborhood of the electric or magnetic bodies." He called his concept a "dynamical theory," because "it assumes that in space there is matter in motion."

At once arose a fascinating question, already provided with some answers: If light is our name for electromagnetic field vibrations at certain frequencies, then what of such vibrations at *other* frequencies?

Maxwell knew that electromagnetic radiation did not begin with the visible red and end with the last violet of the spectrum. Electromagnetic vibrations must extend far beyond the frequencies men knew as "light."

The infra and the ultra. Beyond the last visible red, men could sense with their skins, as heat, radiations which their eyes could not see as light. These were named "infrared," meaning below the red. Instruments and procedures were developed for detecting and measuring the infrared spectrum.

That study still goes on. It is being aided by, and is aiding, the development of masers and lasers.

Today the infrared region is considered to extend from frequencies just below those of red light down all the way to frequencies of about 1×10^{12} cps, equal to a wave length of about ⅓₀₀ cm. The frequency range, or "band width," of this infrared region is about 4×10^{14} cps, or slightly greater than the total band width of the visible light above it.

Above the visible violet, another kind of radiation was known. It was called "ultraviolet," meaning beyond violet. Such rays showed remarkable effects on matter. They were peculiarly potent in affecting photographic plates, causing certain chemical reactions, and bringing about the discharge of charged pieces of metal. Even powerful radiations of light of lesser frequency could not duplicate many of these effects. The higher ultraviolet frequencies must possess powers that cannot be matched by radiations of lower frequency, no matter how intense they might be.

Physicists found that powerful electric-arc and mercury-vapor lights were especially rich in ultraviolet frequencies. Astronomers located distant stars so hot that most of their energy was poured out at frequencies in the ultraviolet rather than in visible light spectrum.

Today the ultraviolet spectrum is known to extend far. It begins just beyond the visible violet, and rises to about 2×10^{17} cps. Its band width thus is about 125 times as great as the combined band widths of infrared and visible light radiations.

Below the infra. Maxwell's epoch-making work pointed convincingly to the possibility of generating or discovering electromagnetic waves at frequencies less than those of infrared and at frequencies higher than those of ultraviolet radiations.

Experiment soon supplied positive evidence. The physicist Heinrich Hertz discovered that by means of high-frequency oscillating electric currents discharged through spark gaps, he

34

could produce "sympathetic" oscillations in similar circuits lying at a distance, even though the latter had not been directly excited by electrical energy.

Clearly, waves of some sort must radiate from the active "transmitter" to the passive "receiver." Such waves were at first called *hertzian* waves. Before long, Marconi and others learned how hertzian waves could be transmitted and detected over distances—ever greater distances.

They spanned the English Channel. Then they spanned the Atlantic Ocean itself, on December 12, 1901. The frequency used was low—3×10^5 cps (300,000 cps), and the wave length 1,000 meters or 10^5 cm. Such were the electromagnetic waves which raced at c, the velocity of light, from Cornwall, England, to Newfoundland, where Marconi himself waited with his crude equipment, his antenna being one wire borne aloft by a kite.

(That kite took its place in science beside the kite which helped Franklin prove the identity between lightning and the electrical discharges generated in his simple laboratory.)

Such hertzian radiations soon became known as "wireless waves," for they eliminated the need for current-carrying wires between transmitter and receiver, which had always been necessary in telegraphy. Today we call them radio waves. The radio section of the electromagnetic spectrum is usually considered to extend from the lowest known frequencies up to those at about 1×10^{10} cps (or about 3 centimeters wave length).

Above these radio frequencies we find the shorter "microwaves" which range up to about 3×10^{11} cps, or a 1-millimeter wave length. These are the microwaves referred to by the word which supplies the first letter of the word *m*aser.

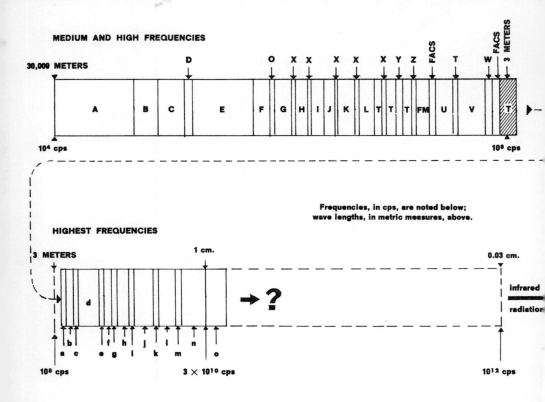

Figure 3.4 Our crowded "airways" in the early 1960s (Assignments of frequency channels from low, at left, to high frequencies, at right.)

KEY (for medium- and high-frequency bands, at top)
(A) Fixed services: point-to-point, high-power, long-wave.
(B) Press, Marine, Coastal, Alaskan, etc.
(C) Maritime beacons, Navigation aids.
(D) Maritime, Ships, Coast, Mobile.
(E) STANDARD BROADCASTING (AM—Amplitude modulation—radio stations)
(F) Police, Aviation, Relay broadcasting
(Facs) Facsimile transmission
(FM) Frequency modulation broadcasting.
(G) Police, Government, Ship, Harbor, Telephone, Forestry, Aero.
(H) Marine, Coastal, etc.

No hard-and-fast division exists between radio and micro-wave frequencies. One section of the spectrum runs into the next. The different names for the different sections are merely matters of convenience. For this reason the use of numerical frequencies is important, so we can know always just where we are in the over-all spectrum.

Wireless communications have moved toward ever higher frequencies. Development of the vacuum tubes and new circuits, the needs of radio telephony (voice and music) as compared with the simpler early telegraphy—all these factors worked to accelerate this shift.

(I) Government, Aviation, etc.
(J) Government, Aviation, Mobile.
(K) Marine, Coastal, Press.
(L) International, Scientific, Medical, etc.
(O) Loran.
(T) Television broadcasting.
(U) Aero, Airport control, Government.
(V) Amateur aviation, Radiosonde, Glide-path Aids, etc.
(X) Amateur ("ham") channels.

KEY (for highest-frequency bands, at bottom)
(a) Experimental broadcast.
(b) Navigation aids.
(c) Amateur.
(d) Television relay, Meteorological (weather), etc.
(e) Amateur
(f) Government, Fixed, Mobile.
(h) Air navigation, etc.
(i) Amateur.
(j) Government & Non-government, Fixed and mobile navigation aids.
(k) Amateur.
(l) Non-government Fixed and mobile, Government.
(m) Amateur.
(n) Government, Non-government.
(o) Experimental.

Finally came the exacting microwave demands of radar, which could work only at very high frequencies.

Today our home radios receive from AM stations at frequencies between about 5×10^5 and 5×10^6 cps. Higher are the bands reserved for police, short-wave transoceanic, and some TV channels. Higher still, between about 8.8×10^7 and 1.1×10^8 cps, lie the FM broadcast channels. Other TV channels are at frequencies above even these (Figure 3.4).

Below microwaves. Where, in fact, do the microwaves come to an end? They do not actually "end." They merely merge into the lowest of the infrared frequencies.

A comic strip some years ago considered the question: Is the smallest giant larger (or smaller) than the biggest dwarf? The same character, it seemed, could do duty for either. The highest-frequency microwaves and the lowest-frequency infrared waves are identical.

In the zone where they meet—around 3×10^{11} to 9×10^{11} cps —the real differences lie in the various *methods* used or proposed for generating these radiations, rather than in the radiations themselves.

Just as the light spectrum is a continuity, one color merging without barrier into the next, so the entire electromagnetic spectrum below light is a continuity. We find great differences in the behavior of the radiations, as we ascend or descend the frequency scale; but there are no barriers, no gaps that man may not hope to bridge in his explorations of the amazing world of radiation.

Above the ultra. An unknown land of radiation remained beyond the ultraviolet. But not for long. Here too the restless march of experimentation filled in the gaps. The physicist W. K. Roentgen, experimenting with beams of electrons shot at high-voltage energy at targets in vacuum tubes, found something unexpected happening. An unknown kind of radiation was emerging. It penetrated flesh or wood with energy enough to register on photographic films or fluorescent screens.

These mysterious radiations were called X *rays,* the X standing for the famous unknown of algebra.

Today we know that the roentgen rays or X rays fit into the electromagnetic radiation spectrum, above the highest frequencies of ultraviolet.

As elsewhere in that great spectrum, the behavior of radiation alters as the frequencies alter. The lower-frequency X rays were found to be less penetrating, less explosive in their effects on matter. They came to be called "soft" X rays. Those higher in the scale, produced only by faster-speeding electrons, are commonly called "hard" X rays.

At these enormous frequencies and vast energies, wave length is rarely used as a measure. Physicists, in fact, find more useful even than the frequency measure another, related to it, known as the "electron volt." It is a measure of energy intensity.

X rays did not prove to be the topmost level of the radiation spectrum. When radioactivity was discovered, it was found to be accompanied by various "rays" resulting from the breakup of atomic nuclei. One type, known as "gamma rays," could not be swerved by a magnetic field. These gamma rays proved to be radiations still higher in the scale of frequency, "hardness," or energy, than X rays themselves.

Later still, studies of surprising radiations and particles reaching the earth from outside the atmosphere revealed even greater energies than in the most powerful gamma rays released by sources on earth. To these radiations from outer

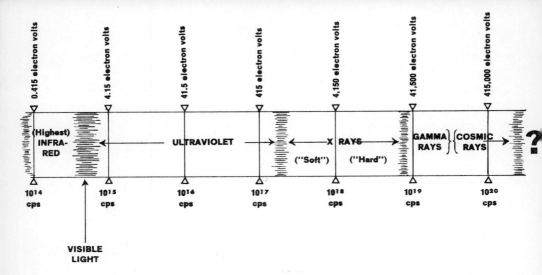

Figure 3.5 The highest-frequency spectrum of radiation from the top of the infrared, at left, to the "hardest" cosmic rays at right.

Scale above shows energy levels in electron volts. Scale below shows frequencies in cycles per second.

space was given the dramatic name "cosmic rays."

Recording devices have registered the arrival of such rays with a degree of hardness or energy corresponding to about 10^{20} cps—or 1000 times greater than the higher ultraviolet radiations.

Here (Figure 3.5) we see the "highest-frequency" spectrum, including the radiations beyond the ultraviolet. (At the bottom is a scale of corresponding frequencies in cps; at the top a scale of energy equivalents in electron volts.)

It is not likely that maser-type devices will operate with radiations of such enormous and violent frequencies. However, the understanding of radiation requires an understanding of the vast range and complete continuity of radiation.

We are better able, with this understanding, to recognize the qualities that all types of radiation have in common.

40

4

RADIATION PATTERNS AND

HUMAN BEINGS

THE SCALE of radiation is so vast that it may make us a little dizzy. We have followed it through to the seemingly explosive "bullets" of cosmic rays, equivalent to 10^{20} cps. And at the opposite extreme you can find electromagnetic radiations with frequencies as low as 6×10 cps.

In fact, you are receiving such frequencies every time your auto radio picks up a hum from high-tension wires. These alternate—oscillate—at 60 cps. The corresponding wave length is consequently about 3,200 miles long!

Would you like to compare the frequency of the "hardest" cosmic ray with that of the high-tension wire's radiations? The former is about 1.7×10^{19} times the latter! And 10^{19} is 10 times a million times a million times a million!

Yet we can see that even these extremes have certain qualities in common:

(1) *Velocity*—All radiation travels with a velocity of c

(3×10^{10} cm.) through empty space.

(2) *Continuity*—There are no sharp walls or jumps between radiation of any definite frequency and radiation of slightly higher or lesser frequency.

(3) *Identification*—The behavior of any definite radiation, with regard to the matter that emits or absorbs it, remains constant. Like situations always produce like results. If you define the frequency and the intensity of a radiation, its effects can be predicted on the basis of past experience.

Now for a most important addition. A very great Danish physicist and pioneer of atomic study, Niels Bohr—whose death is announced just as these lines are being written—gave this memorable, short definition:

"[Radiation is] the transmission of energy between material bodies at a distance."

Energy is the ability to do work. Radiation and energy are thus inseparable.

(4) *Matterless energy in motion*—Radiation is a transport of energy, minus matter, at the speed of light.

Except for radiation there is no way to transport energy from one bit of matter to another. And there is no way to make matter, or even its tiniest particles, move as fast as light. This was predicted in Einstein's relativity theories. Today it is common knowledge among engineers who work with powerful electron tubes and physicists who use particle accelerators, such as cyclotrons, synchrotrons, and linear accelerators.

Electrons, when very energetically pushed, can be forced to velocities very close to that of light and other radiation. But they can never be brought quite up to the rate of c.

Radiation, in its relationship to matter and energy, remains unique and unapproachable. So, too, in its velocity. Radiation

Niels Bohr

is truly something basic, fundamental, and "special."

(5) *Origin in matter*—Radiation is always launched from matter. Such a launching or emission always represents a shift of energy. Matter loses energy—and a corresponding amount of energy flies off at the speed c in the form we call radiation.

(6) *Termination in matter*—Radiation ceases to be, only when its energy once again becomes a part of matter. When radiation reaches matter which takes in (absorbs) its energy,

43

the matter gains energy and a corresponding amount of radiation is wiped out.

Notice that energy is not "lost" or "wasted." It is merely transferred and transformed. Energy is never lost. That is one of the basic laws of nature.

(7) *The matterless transfer of energy from matter to matter* summarizes the important aspect of radiation. Radiation is the only way that one material body can give energy to another—except by contact.

Such contacts are usually collisions of one sort or another. Thus, a rolling billiard ball may transfer energy of motion to a stationary one. Or a glowing electric coil may pass molecular energy (heat) to the saucepan that rests on it. Or the motion energy in wind is transmitted to a boat by means of its sail. Or the chemical energy locked in fuel, released by the reaction of burning, becomes motion or mechanical energy of particles rushing out of the nozzle, and thus motion or mechanical energy of the rocket or jet plane. All such energy transfers involve direct contacts of body with body, particle with particle.

We can see radiation as a kind of storage, in space, of speeding energy. Much distance and time may separate the original emission and the final absorption of a quantity of radiation. Yet it goes on through space, unwasting, unchanging in velocity, unchanging in frequency, until absorbed.

What we know of radiation, we know because of its effects on matter. It is like the wind in this respect—we cannot see the transparent air blow past us, but we see the dust it stirs, the leaves it blows, the boughs it shakes. . . .

Matter responds with changes only to those radiations to which it is tuned. This is true of the tiny structures of particles which we call atoms, the structures of atoms which we call

44

molecules, and the collections of atoms and molecules which we call material bodies, whether solid, liquid, or gas. It is true also of the radiation receivers of living things, ears and eyes.

The wood of a house shows no obvious change as a result of the radio waves that pass freely through it. Yet its temperature goes up when it is bombarded by infrared radiations from the sun.

Our eyes do not respond to microwaves. We cannot sense X rays with our skin, though later much damage may result.

The radar receiver does not respond to light, nor the photographic film to radio broadcasting.

The substances and structures that will respond to radiation with measurable changes differ according to the frequency of the radiation. Likewise the substances, structures, or devices that will emit radiation in one frequency range differ from those that will emit radiation in another range.

Thus radiation must always be studied in terms of its interaction with matter and material structures. There is no other way to approach it.

Radiation can reveal the inmost secrets of matter. The growth of science has been largely a growth in man's ability to receive, measure, and interpret radiation.

A century ago the existence of natural radiations in microwave frequencies was hardly suspected. Yet today radioastronomers with their vast receiver telescopes gather and study such radiation, which streams in constantly from outer space, as it has always done. There is, for example, important radiation near the frequency of 7×10^{10} cps. It is emitted by "cold" atoms of hydrogen as they undergo certain energy changes in space.

Development of improved receivers, sensitive to such frequencies, has greatly increased man's knowledge of the cosmos. Masers, too, are aiding in receiving and reading these naturally occurring radiations.

At the top of the known spectrum of radiation, the cosmic rays tell a similar story. They have streamed in on the earth since before recorded history began, yet only after men developed instruments with suitable sensitivity could these violent visitors from space be identified, counted, and measured.

Radiation as man's messenger. Men read natural radiations and learn deep-rooted secrets of nature.

Men also make use of radiation to communicate among themselves. An endless and ever growing flood of messages is carried by means of radiations in the radio and microwave frequencies.

These include private messages from person to person or small group to group. They include the great "mass messages" of broadcast radio and television.

Some of the messages are spoken words, some are music, some are pictures, some are commands to satellites orbiting the earth or flying toward the moon or the sun. Some are reports from such satellites back to earth.

Some of the messages are information about location, shape, and size (as in radar).

And some of these man-made, radiation-carried messages are replies that are given by atoms and molecules that have been "questioned" by scientists using radiations designed to probe matter's inmost structures and behaviors.

Man's use of radiation in communication has grown with fantastic swiftness during the past few decades. Yet, when we check the full radiation spectrum, we find that until now men have been able to make use of only a small part of its frequency range.

In fact, men have been able—until masers—to generate radiations suited to their communications needs only at frequencies below about 3×10^{11} cps.

Above this level, there seemed no way to generate radiations suited to the requirements of human communications. Infrared, visible light, ultraviolet and the rest were almost useless so far as modern communications methods are concerned.

Certainly light is used in human communication, but in another sense. Without light neither this book nor any magazine, newspaper, letter or other written communication could ever be read. Light carries to our eyes the letter patterns on which written communication is based, just as sound waves carry to our ears the acoustical patterns which form spoken language. Of that there is no doubt.

However, men use radio and microwaves as messengers for their communication in a very different way. Radio broadcasting, television, radar and the rest are possible because, and only because, we have devices able to generate pure, powerful, and "coherent" radiations in those frequencies. Such radiation serves as the carrier, or messenger. It bears the myriads of different messages that men entrust to it or impress upon it.

Men could generate artificially radiations of light, heat (infrared), ultraviolet and the rest, but before lasers they could not generate these with sufficient purity, power, and coherence to serve as carriers of communications.

Let us look at the qualifications of a modern short-wave radio transmitter such as may send out your favorite TV programs.

(1) *It is powerful.* Such a transmitter can radiate 10 or 15 thousand watts of power at various frequencies in its range. (1000 watts = 1 kilowatt)

(2) *It is pure and precise.* This full radiated power can be concentrated within a frequency band, or band width, as narrow as 1×10^6 cps (one megacycle). For example, if the central frequency is, say, 6×10^7, no apparent radiation will be emitted outside the limits set by half a megacycle above and half a megacycle below that central frequency (Figure 4.1). The carrier wave emitted by such a transmitter is uniform, continuous, and steady. It is, in a word we shall meet again, highly "coherent."

Actual TV transmission requires a band width about 4 megacycles wide to carry all the complicated details of the constantly changing pictures. The channel assigned to each station must have sufficient "elbow room" so the station will not crowd or interfere with other stations operating in the area.

For these reasons, the present frequency bands reserved for TV will permit only a rather limited number of channels to be used in a single area.

In contrast, about 15 million separate TV channels could operate in the frequency range of light between the center of the spectrum's red area (about 423×10^{14} cps) and the center of the orange (483×10^{14} cps)—if such light radiation could be generated as coherently and powerfully as are radio waves today.

Another necessary quality of modern radio transmission—

(3) *It is not noisy.* "Noise" is a very special word for communications engineers and scientists. It does not refer to the content of TV shows or singing commercials. It means irregular, unpredictable, random radiations, or unwanted signals that are mixed in with the wanted ones.

Excess noise in a room or hall may drown out the speaker

48

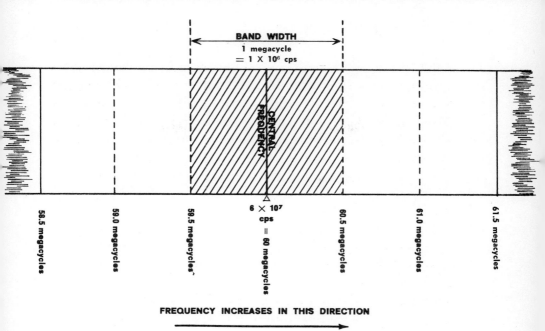

BAND WIDTH
1 megacycle
$= 1 \times 10^6$ cps

CENTRAL FREQUENCY

6×10^7 cps
$= 60$ megacycles

58.5 megacycles · 59.0 megacycles · 59.5 megacycles · 60.5 megacycles · 61.0 megacycles · 61.5 megacycles

FREQUENCY INCREASES IN THIS DIRECTION

Figure 4.1 Band width—a limited range of frequencies. (Shaded area shows a band width of 1 megacycle (a million cycles) centered around a frequency of 60 megacycles, or 6 x 10⁷ cps. TV transmission requires a band width about four times as great.)

you seek to hear. Excess noise in a transmitter—or a receiver —swamps the signal that it should bring to your ears or eyes.

Noise may appear in a radio as hissing, frying, crackling, rumbling, etc. It may appear on a TV screen as "snow" or "rain."

Turning up the control marked "volume" or "gain" only increases the level of noise. If you amplify all the sound received in a noisy room, you amplify the noise as well as the message you want to hear.

In the earliest days of wireless telegraphy, transmitters

49

made use of spark gaps. (Vacuum tubes came later.) Their transmitted waves were noisy and irregular. They were suited, at best, to carry the simpler information of dots and dashes (Morse-code telegraphy). They could not carry the complicated and subtle information that we receive as voice, music, and pictures.

The modern radio and microwave transmitter must be virtually free from noise. This is implied when we say that its carrier wave must be "coherent."

These three requirements for a satisfactory transmitter were not satisfied by the devices men had developed to emit light and the invisible radiations in infrared and ultraviolet. They were not satisfied either by the natural sources of such radiations. Let us take light as the easiest example.

The sun, before lasers appeared, seemed the source of the most intense, concentrated radiations available to man. Its radiations cover an enormous range of frequencies, from deep down in infrared, through light, to far into ultraviolet.

Suppose we eliminate, by means of filters, all solar radiation excepting that in a rather narrow frequency band width—say, 1 megacycle wide, as mentioned before. Let us choose it in the blue-green part of the spectrum, around 625×10^{14} cps, where the sun's spectrum shows its greatest energy concentration.

We find that the power of radiation within this restricted band width of 1 megacycle is actually quite low. In fact, even at the sun's surface we would have to sift the total radiation of an area of 10 square meters in order to gather 1 watt of power within that 1 megacycle band.

In other words, a modern man-made TV transmitter, by means of its oscillating currents, emits as much power in a 1-megacycle range as do 100,000 square meters of the sun's surface, which has a temperature of some 6000° C!

The total power radiated by the sun is enormous. However, the segment of power that falls within any band width likely to be useful in human communications is tiny. Its radiation is diffused, not precise. It is not powerful in any narrow frequency range.

Suppose you needed many rivets of a certain size. Store A might have a stock of 10 million rivets, with only half a dozen in the size you need. Store B might have only 5000 rivets in stock, but 2000 of these are in your size. You would certainly do better at Store B.

Most of the man-made sources of light exhibit disadvantages similar to those of the sun. They make matter become incandescent by releasing its energy through combustion—oil, wax (candles), gas. Fire makes matter hot. Molecules dance and vibrate every which way. Most vibrate at rates which radiate heat (infrared). Some atoms become excited enough to radiate light.

Electric currents make possible light sources which are far more powerful (arcs, for instance) and convenient (tungsten-filament bulbs) and even less wasteful of energy in heat (neon and fluorescent-tube lights). But basically all of these sources generate light which is mixed in frequencies, discontinuous, and incoherent.

Here are two contrasting pictures of wave motion. The first (Figure 4.2) represents the carrier wave emitted by a modern radio transmitter during a moment of silence. It is uniform, steady, coherent. The second (Figure 4.3) represents the light emitted by almost any source you can name (other than a laser). It is irregular, mixed, composed of bits and pieces differing in their frequencies, differing in their direc-

51

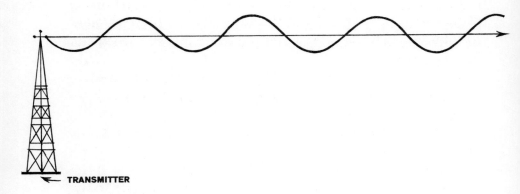

TRANSMITTER

Figure 4.2 Coherent radiation—the carrier wave emitted by a modern radio transmitter. (Uniform in frequency, in amplitude, and continuous—not broken into bits and pieces.)

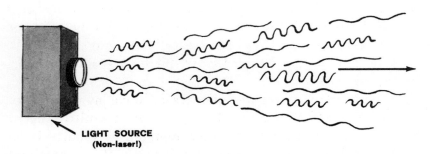

LIGHT SOURCE
(Non-laser!)

Figure 4.3 Incoherent radiation (somewhat exaggerated, for clarity)—the beam emitted by all light sources before the lasers. (Unlike in frequencies, in amplitude, and duration.) Such beams are bound to spread as they travel out from their sources. They cannot be kept strictly parallel.

tions, and differing in their durations. In short, it is *incoherent*.

Incoherent radiation is necessarily "noisy" radiation. It cannot serve as a carrier for the information that men need to communicate. The starts, the stops, the shifts in frequency —without pattern or predictability—all these render it unfit.

Moreover, incoherent radiation cannot be intensely concentrated in space. Neither lenses nor curved reflectors will focus incoherent radiation within a tiny point of energy. True, you can focus the sun's rays with a lens or burning glass and kindle a fire. But there are limits on the energy concentration which can be achieved in this way.

Only coherent light can be held parallel as it travels, in a pencil beam. Only coherent radiation can avoid great spreading out and dilution of energy as it travels through space away from its source. Only with coherent radiation, finally, can we achieve interference effects between one beam and another.

Such interference is, in fact, the test for, and the proof of, true coherence. Glance again at Figures 2.2 and 2.3 on page 22, showing the famous Young interference experiment. Notice that only one beam from the lamp is divided and then caused to recombine. That beam *interferes* with itself. Had one slit transmitted the beam from this lamp and the other slit a beam from another lamp, no interference fringes would form. The waves from one lamp would be too incoherent, too "out of step," with those from the other.

We cannot cause interference even by using beams of light taken from different parts of the same lamp flame or filament. Such emitters of light operate chaotically and incoherently. Their molecules lack unanimity. They radiate spontaneously, separately, and unpredictably.

Which way to coherent light? Why not build miniature versions of microwave transmitters—so small that they emit wave lengths of coherent infrared or visible light?

This is unfortunately impossible. Miniaturizing has gone a long way in recent years, but not a thousandth of the way that would be necessary for this. The smaller transmitter elements become, the less power they can handle. Our radio and microwave transmitters depend on oscillating surges of electrons for their electromagnetic radiations. A transmitter so tiny that it could handle relatively few electrons would produce waves correspondingly weak.

Communications engineers and inventors showed enormous ingenuity. They devised radically new kinds of electron controllers—tubes with names such as "magnetrons," "klystrons," "traveling-wave tubes," etc.

But by the closing years of the 1940s it began to seem that even these were reaching limits in the drive toward ever shorter microwaves.

Meanwhile the higher frequencies beckoned like a promised land. Here was the added room, the band-width space that human communicators craved. But how to enter in?

The key would have to be some way to achieve coherent and controllable radiations at frequencies far higher than could be attained and sustained by any man-made circuit, tube, or resonator.

The key was found, else there could be no such book as this about masers and lasers. It was found along a road that led through provoking problems to unexpected solutions.

The initial section of this road merits a name like a detective story—"The Dilemma of the Violet Catastrophe."

5

THE DILEMMA

OF THE VIOLET CATASTROPHE

THE ATOMS and molecules that compose matter are too tiny for us to visualize. Scientists can state quite exactly how many molecules must be bouncing about in 1 cubic centimeter of gas at a certain temperature and pressure. But no one can picture in "everyday" human terms just what goes on in that submicroscopic world.

For this reason we must approach masers and lasers step by step.

Molecules of matter, we know, are constantly moving. Any moving matter, however tiny, has energy because it moves. The faster it moves, the greater that energy becomes. Energy is the ability to do work. The faster a particle flies, the more work it can do.

Matter appears in several states—solid, liquid, gas. We know that by adding or taking away energy we can change a substance from one state to another. Some of that energy may

55

remain in the matter at times as energy of position (potential energy). Other parts of the energy appear as energy of motion (kinetic energy) of the particles.

Let us start with a cold solid and gradually add energy (heat it). The molecules of the solid vibrate and jiggle around positions more or less fixed in its over-all structure. As they gain energy they vibrate faster, and over wider paths. Finally they begin to slide past each other. We who watch say, "The solid is melting and becoming liquid."

We continue to heat the liquid. Its molecules bounce and move ever more energetically. Some, acquiring sufficient speed, break away from the mass and fly past the surface (evaporate). More and more follow. Finally all are flying, colliding, bounding about at random, penetrating every possible space in their container.

We who continue to watch describe this change by saying, "The liquid has boiled away and become a vapor, or gas."

The energy we added or "injected" in each case probably took a familiar form—outside heat, transmitted to the molecules either by contact (conduction) or by radiation. Usually some of each is involved.

The reverse changes can take place too. Suppose we withdraw energy—another name for cooling the gas. The average velocity of its molecules is reduced. They begin to cluster and slide about one another again. *Condensation* has begun. Continued cooling will liquefy all the gas.

Withdraw still more energy of motion from the molecules (let them cool further). Their energies are no longer great enough to resist forces which seek to pull them into fixed structural relations. Freezing sets in. In many substances it takes the form of crystallization. What was liquid has become a regular solid.

Underlying these changes of state are the changes in energies of the particles making up the matter. Some energy changes are reflected in the changed energy of position or structure—comparable to the energy stored in the spring of a watch spring that has been wound. Other energy shows itself because of the motion of the particles making up the gas, liquid, or solid. This last is the kinetic or motion energy.

It is an average of such motion energy that we know under the name of "temperature." Scientists work mostly with a scale that sets zero as far down as possible—to the point where, it was once believed, matter lost all its energy. This "absolute zero" is a little more than 273° below the centigrade zero, which is at the freezing point of water.

The absolute scale is named after the scientist Lord Kelvin, and is indicated by the letter K, as C indicates centigrade. We can recall that water freezes near 273° K, boils near 373° K at sea level; and what we call "room temperature" is near 300° K.

Temperature and radiation. If you switch on an electric heater or the coil of an electric stove, its temperature begins at once to rise. The molecules of its metal are agitated and buffeted by great surges of electrons, which we call electric current.

Hold your hand near—but not too near! You soon feel warmth radiating from the heated metal. Energy is streaming out, radiant energy.

If temperature continues to climb, your eyes too begin to notice this radiated energy, for the metal begins to glow a dull red. This becomes brighter and lighter. A red-hot point is reached in time. If the current is strong enough, radiation energy continues to climb the frequency scale, and cherry red gives way to something brighter and lighter still.

No need to risk melting an electric heater or stove unit. Simply watch the tungsten wire in a light bulb when you turn it on. In a split second it radiates that complex mixture of frequencies which most of us call "white light."

And the radiation from a powerful electric arc or mercury-vapor lamp, you will find, is even richer than the tungsten bulb in the high frequencies of blue and violet.

Scientists early found one significant difference, and one very significant sameness. Some substances, like tungsten, remained solids even at white heat. Others melted even before they became red-hot. There was no single temperature pattern regarding change of state.

But there was this sameness: all substances, whatever their state at the time, seemed to become red-hot at the same temperature and white-hot at the same temperature. In fact, by carefully noting the radiated color, you could make a fairly good guess as to the temperature of the substance, whether it was iron, brass, gold, silver, or perhaps a mixture known as glass.

Clearly, close connections existed between (1) temperature, and (2) the frequencies at which energy was radiated.

During the nineteenth century these connections were studied carefully and completely. Some of the results help us here along the road to masers and lasers.

Scientists found they could learn most by working with the most complete and consistent form of radiation. They called it "black-body" equilibrium radiation. It is emitted at a steady temperature by a body which is a perfect radiator at all frequencies. Such a body must also be a perfect absorber for all frequencies, for a good radiator is always a good absorber, a poor radiator a poor absorber.

A body with a shiny, light surface is a poor radiator and poor absorber of radiations. One with a dull-black surface is a good radiator and absorber. The ideal that scientists sought was a substance which at any temperature would radiate and absorb all frequencies perfectly.

There was no such substance. But there was a way to imitate one by means of a rather simple trick of construction.

Figure 5.1 shows a mass of metal. It can be heated to, and held at, any of many different temperatures. A cavity, C, has been formed in it. This cavity is always full of the radiations emitted by the metal at its prevailing temperature.

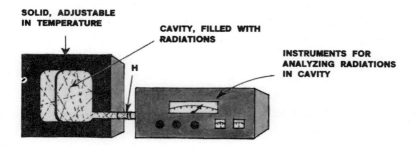

Figure 5.1 Artificial black-body for studying radiation patterns at various temperatures.

These radiations cannot escape from the cavity. (The hole, H, provided for sampling and measuring the radiations is so small that it scarcely matters.) Hence the radiations bounce back and forth from and to the walls of the cavity until, sooner or later, all are absorbed in those walls. Meantime the walls send out more radiation. And so it goes.

The cavity radiation acts like perfect black-body radiation. Its energy distribution at any steady temperature of the metal is typical of that temperature. It is not influenced by the material in which the cavity is formed. Its pattern never changes so long as the temperature is held steady. And whenever the temperature is brought back to that point later on, the same radiation pattern appears.

These cavity devices served as a kind of Aladdin's lamp. They conjured up much important new knowledge—and also some unexpected problems which loomed like glowering genii over puzzled investigators.

Here are some of these basic radiation facts:

(1) Each body constantly emits and absorbs radiations. This goes on even at what we call "low" temperatures. Example: at about 200° K, or about 73° below water's freezing point, more than 90 watts of power constantly radiate from a dull-black iron surface one meter square. Even at 100° K—or 173° below centigrade's zero—the rate is more than 5 watts.

(2) Bodies of matter reach and keep the same temperatures as bodies around them. They do this not because they *stop* emitting and absorbing radiation, but because they absorb just as much energy as they emit, and emit as much as they absorb. Radiation never ceases. It operates so as to equalize temperature differences between bodies. It is a constant two-way process.

(3) For each temperature of matter, there is a characteristic pattern of radiation. A single temperature is not just one number on a scale. It is, rather, a particular measurable and describable way in which energy is distributed among various radiation wave lengths or frequencies.

Figure 5.2 shows the patterns for five temperatures, from

60

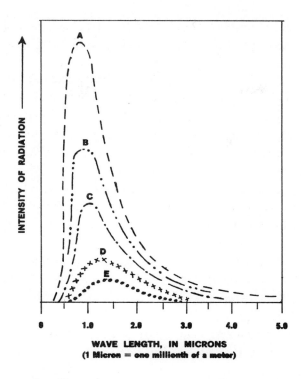

Figure 5.2 Radiation patterns formed in thermal equilibrium at various typical temperatures.
Key: A—at 3655°, B—at 3300°, C—at 2970°, D—at 2500°, E—at 2150°, all on Kelvin scale.

2150° to 3655° K. We see that the peak of energy moves to shorter wave lengths—meaning higher frequencies—as temperature goes up.

Also we see that each curve covers a greater area than the ones below it. This suggests the following important fact:

(4) As temperature rises, the rate of total energy radiation

61

rises far more steeply. For the perfect black-body radiator, the increase is proportional to the *fourth power* of temperature on the absolute K scale.

For example, if you found such a body radiated 1 watt of power at 100° K, you would see that power soar as temperature was raised: 16 watts at 200°; 81 at 300°; 256 at 400°; 625 at 500°; 1296 at 600°; 2401 at 700°; 4096 at 800°; 6561 at 900°; 10,000 watts at 100°; 14,461 at 1100°; 20,736 at 1200° K; and so on.

Vast amounts of energy, it seems, are emitted in the form of radiation by hot matter. Equally vast amounts of energy are absorbed when such matter is in a state of thermal equilibrium with the surrounding radiation.

But science must pierce through appearances. Are these amounts of radiated energy really large? How do they compare with the total energy that exists in the matter *and* in the radiation-filled space?

Scientists computed how much energy must be contained, at a typical instant, in one cubic centimeter of such space, and how much in one cubic centimeter of the hot metal. The difference was enormous. For example, at 1200° K any bit of the hot metal held about 1.3×10^{12} times as much energy as the same volume of the radiation-filled cavity.

This is a difference of more than a million *times* a million!

Why did energy remain so stubbornly associated with substance? Why did so little of it leave matter, and return to matter, in the form of radiation? Why was energy so concentrated in substance, so extremely diluted in space?

Accepted theories of matter motion and radiation could not supply sensible answers. Sir James Jeans, an eloquent student of radiation problems, offered a vivid picture to illustrate what "should" happen but does not. . . .

Here (Figure 5.3) is a swimming pool full of water. You make an elastic net and where its cords cross, you fasten cork floats. You attach this net over the pool so its corks rest quietly on the surface of the water (Figure 5.4).

Figure 5.3   Figure 5.4

Now you poke the corks to make them bob up and down. Thus you give them motion energy. The result is clear: they form waves and ripples in the water. These waves travel from cork to cork. They reflect back from the sides of the pool. Soon the water is filled with waves going back and forth.

Then, more or less gradually, the disturbances die down, leaving the corks once again quietly floating on quiet water. If you used a very sensitive thermometer, you would find the water in the pool just a bit warmer as a result of the molecular (heat) motion now scattered through it.

In other words, energy that was in moving corks and stretched elastic cords is now in the water.

In this model the corks and cords represent the solid body, its molecules tied together, yet able to vibrate more or less independently. The water in the pool represents the space filled with radiation. When a bobbing cork makes a wave, this stands for an emission of radiation. When a wave shakes a cork, this stands for an absorption of radiation.

So far, a fairly good mechanical analogy. But what a difference in final outcome! In this model the energy passed entirely into the water (space). In actual radiation experiments only a tiny part of the total energy is found at any time in space. Almost all is in the matter.

Sir James noted that no one could imagine a final situation in which "the water had no energy while the corks continued to oscillate with extreme vigor."

Yet just this was happening in black-body radiators, and always and everywhere in the endless interchanges between matter and energy. Why?

The radiation theories which then prevailed suggested there should be a constant shifting of ever increasing amounts of available energy into radiations at ever higher frequencies. This shift *should* go on unchecked, accelerating, up through the green, the blue, the violet, and higher frequencies.

The end—according to these theories—should come only when matter was quite cold, drained of heat energy, while space was filled with a vast burst of blinding radiation. There was even a name for this imaginary event which did *not* take place. It was called "the violet catastrophe."

Why did it not happen?

How could theories, seemingly so well grounded in mathematics and logic and the knowledge of how electromagnetic waves were formed and propagated, be so far from the facts?

Such was the dilemma that confronted scientists as the nineteenth century drew to its close. Among them was a particularly thorough, patient, and persistent physicist. His name was Max Planck. And to him belongs the following chapter.

6

THE KEY CALLED THE QUANTUM

MAX PLANCK was inspired by a deep desire for consistency. He did not fear that a cosmic "violet catastrophe" was just around the corner. But he wanted to eliminate this contradiction, and another that was related to it:

No single mathematical formula had been found which accurately described how radiation patterns formed at various temperatures in the cavity. One formula, identified with a scientist named Wien, fitted the observed facts for high frequencies and low temperatures, but differed annoyingly from results found at low frequencies and high temperatures. Another, known as the Rayleigh-Jeans formula, worked well for low frequencies and high temperatures, but was very far off for high frequencies.

Planck set out to find a reconciliation. He did find it—but to do so he was compelled to make a supposition so novel, so at variance with all that had been accepted in science before 1900, that he never quite reconciled himself to all its consequences.

Dr. Chen Ning Yang, a recent Nobel prize winner in physics, has written that a concept "so revolutionary . . . could only have originated from the thoroughness and persistence that characterized Planck's studies."

Someday you may judge for yourself, in Planck's book which in English bears the title *The Theory of Heat Radiation*. It still makes fascinating reading for the relatively few able to understand its mathematics and technical approach.

We shall approach Planck's concept by analogies rather than mathematics. In dealing with the processes of emission and absorption of radiation, it is often convenient to use comparisons that have to do with money—with income and expenditures, with profit and loss.

Suppose you operate a small business, such as a lemonade stand. Think of what you spend as your "emissions" of radiation, what you take in as your "absorption." Now, if you spend more than you take in, you lose money—that is, you lose energy and become cooler. In fact, if this goes on long enough, you will be "frozen out" of the business world.

If you take in more than you spend, however, you make a profit. That is, you grow warmer.

However, if your income and your expenditures just balance, you are in equilibrium. Your temperature remains constant. So too does the flow of emissions and absorptions.

The expenditures of "hot-body" businesses observed in the laboratories seemed strangely low to scientists just before 1900, as mentioned before. This was noted especially with regard to the amounts of energy radiated at the highest frequencies.

To make clearer how Planck proposed to solve this problem,

let us improve our business model a little. Each unit of matter —molecule or atom, as the case may be—we shall think of as a small business. The amount of money in the cash drawer will represent the energy an atom has available at the moment. After each day's business, the atom merchant makes a deposit in his bank. That deposit stands for an emission of radiation, and so the bank represents space around the atom.

The profits of these merchants *average* one hundred dollars a day. This would give us an idea of the average energy or temperature level. Some merchants, however, will have larger profits, some smaller profits, on any day. And the same merchant may one day profit more, and another day less, than a hundred dollars.

Now suppose that at the end of each day each merchant deposited in the bank whatever had accumulated in his cash drawer. Then the cash would all flow to the bank. None would remain in the businesses. It would be like the "violet catastrophe" with the energy all radiating into space, leaving matter cold and energyless.

Now what Planck proposed was that the rules regarding matter and radiation must be quite different.

"Supposing," he said in effect (for he certainly did *not* use such an analogy) "supposing a merchant could make a deposit in the bank only when the sum accumulated in his cash drawer was one thousand dollars . . ."

It appears that the average merchant would then make deposits less often. Less often, in fact, than once every ten days on the average. Thus, though individual deposits might be bigger, the average per day of such deposits would be less than one hundred dollars for each merchant.

The result would be that the merchants, taken as a group,

would have more money in their cash drawers. In other words, more energy would remain in matter, less would radiate.

And this was just what careful observation showed did take place.

In the example just given, there is a least sum which can be deposited (emitted as a radiation). It is the energy quantity or *quantum* in which any such emission must take place.

Planck gave this name *quantum* to the smallest possible energy unit which can be radiated at any specific frequency. (The plural of *quantum* is *quanta*.) He did not invent the word, but the concept he attached to it truly revolutionized modern science. That revolution has not yet run its course. The maser and the laser are only two of many great episodes in that continuing revolution.

Planck showed that energy as well as matter must be *atomic* in its structure. There is a least possible unit of energy for each frequency of radiation. This quantum is directly proportional to the frequency. Thus, if the frequency doubles, the energy content of the quantum must double.

The proportion between the frequency (expressed in cps) and the amount of energy bundled up in a quantum is a proportion which is always and everywhere the same. It is, like the velocity of light, a constant.

Planck showed that this constant, which is now represented by the letter h, is expressed in this simple relationship:

$$e = h \times f$$

where e is the energy in a quantum of radiation, and f is the frequency at which that energy is radiated.

This may seem simple enough. It is.

It may also seem reasonable enough—today.

However, some sixty years ago it was upsetting, to say the

least. The accepted theory went like this: Light was recognized as electromagnetic waves. They spread out in space from the source which emitted them. The intensity of a steady beam of light diminished as the square of the distance from the source. If you received 1 unit of red light energy per second, say, on a square centimeter of surface at a distance of 1 meter, you would receive 0.01 units of energy on the same area at a distance of 10 meters, 0.0001 units at 100 meters, and so on.

By going far enough away, you could reduce your energy reception as low as you liked. That was what the pre-quantum concepts assumed. . . .

But Planck's quantum meant that you could never at any instant receive red light of less energy than that of the quantum: $h \times f$. You might in one second receive *no* such quantum, or *one*, or *two*, or *any whole number* of quanta. But you could never receive less than one, nor could you receive a whole number plus a fraction. Quanta could not be cut. They could not be added to. They were the indivisible atoms of energy. Their size was set by their frequency.

The constant h—known, fittingly, as "Planck's constant"—has been measured quite exactly. It is continually used, in all sorts of basic measurements of physics. Like c, the velocity of light, h requires many zeros to write it out in full. But these are zeros after the decimal point, for h is an *extremely* small number.

It *must* be small, for it represents the ratio between a very small numerator, e (the energy carried by a single unit of radiation), and a very large denominator, f (the frequency of that radiation in cps.): $h = e/f$.

Atoms are incredibly tiny. Hence the amount of energy any one of them can emit, or absorb, at a time, must be tiny too.

69

Also, since atoms are tiny, the size—wave length—of their electromagnetic vibrations must be tiny, and the frequency correspondingly high.

Thus we find that according to late results, h equals about 6.625×10^{-27} erg seconds. That is a shorthand way of writing this tiny decimal:

0.000 000 000 000 000 000 000 000 006 625 erg seconds.

Since h expresses a proportion between energy, measured in ergs, and frequency, measured in cycles per second, h itself must represent both energy (ergs) and time (seconds). This energy-time combination is sometimes called "action" by scientists, so h is often known as "Planck's constant of action."

Unchanging proportions are used continually by all of us. Example: 12 is the unchanging proportion between the length of a foot and an inch; 5,280 between the length of a mile and a foot; 63,600 between the length of a mile and an inch.

Also $2,925 \times 10^{15}$ is the proportion to use if you ever need to know how many centimeters light travels in a day (twenty-four hours).

Conversely: 1/12 is the proportion between the length of an inch and a foot. Thus $1/12 \times 48 = 4$ tells us there are 4 feet in 48 inches.

And Planck's h tells us how much energy there must be in the smallest possible unit or quantum of radiation of a certain frequency. Planck's h is far more basic than these other proportions. It is well worth our attention. . . .

How to use Planck's h. Even without mathematics, we can see that this little h has a very big effect on what goes on all around us all the time. It means that the higher the frequency (or the shorter the wave length) of radiation, the larger the size of the packages in which radiation's energy is delivered.

70

We have seen that the violet light at the top of the visible spectrum has just about double the frequency of the red light at the bottom. So we know that violet light comes always in quanta about twice as large as those of the red. (Does this suggest any reason why violet light is especially active in promoting certain chemical reactions that are in no way aided by red? Or why your skin may tan under violet and ultraviolet rays but show no such reaction to red and infrared?

Another example: If we go high enough up the scale of frequencies, we find that certain "hard" X rays have energies, or frequency equivalents, 10,000 times those of red light. These X-ray quanta must each carry 10,000 times the energy of a red-light quantum. (What can one say about the potency of such "hard" X rays and their effects on living tissue and organic substances?)

Higher still, we find the gamma radiations released by radioactive processes or nuclear decay. The least-possible energy unit here is even larger—nearly 100,000 times as large as the quantum of red light. (Does this tell us anything about the possible harm to human cells, and human heredity, of even "a few" such quanta added to the normal or usual background levels?)

Truly, tiny h is one of the great keys to the wonder-evoking and unexpected natural world in which we live. We are going to see something of what this key accomplished in the hands of Albert Einstein. . . .

7

EINSTEIN EXPLORES EMISSIONS

PLANCK used his quantum concept cautiously. He hesitated to extend it far. Einstein was bolder. In a series of brilliant papers beginning in 1905 he applied the quantum concept to one important problem of physics after another. In each case it seemed to work wonders. Long-standing puzzles were solved.

At the same time Einstein was extending his relativity theories. Thus he was leading in the two greatest advances of modern science—quantum theory and relativity.

With the quantum key Einstein opened the door to the road that recently has led to masers and lasers. The date of that opening can be fixed very exactly. It was a paper by Einstein, published first in 1916 in Zurich, Switzerland, and again in 1917 in Berlin, Germany.

The title in English is "On the Quantum Theory of Radiation." There is no mention in it of a maser or of any device that even resembles one. But just as Maxwell's electromagnetic equations pointed the way for radio waves, so Einstein's work on quantum radiation pointed the way to maser action.

One of the many tributes attesting to this is that of Professor R. A. Smith, a British specialist in radiation problems:

"It is amazing how many scientific developments have sprung from ideas originated by Einstein. . . . The fundamental ideas on which (masers and lasers) are based were introduced by Einstein in his discussion of the acute problems that arose in the early days of the quantum theory of radiation."

Einstein emphasized that the radiation quanta acted like moving particles. He gave them a name to emphasize this: *photons.* This name has stuck to the present day. It emphasizes (in the syllable *"phot"*) that these are units of *light,* and (in the syllable *"on"*) that each is a particle, comparable to an electr*on.*

Electrons have negative charge; photons have *no* charge. Moving electrons have energy, the amount depending on how fast they are made to move. Photons are always in motion at the speed c. They have energy, the amount depending (according to $e = h \times f$) on the frequency, f, of the electromagnetic waves to which they correspond.

Einstein had shown that energy and mass were equivalent ($E = mc^2$). Hence the energy of a photon must act like mass. It can be measured by $M = h f/c^2$, where M is the mass in grams, f the frequency in cps, and h and c the familiar constants we have met before.

When a mass moves, it has momentum—the product of its mass times its velocity. Thus a mass of 2 pounds moving at a rate of 10 feet per second has a momentum of 20 foot-pounds per second. A photon moves at the velocity c. Hence

Figure 7.1 Atom man is driven back by the impact of the photon ball. (Absorption means transfer of momentum from the absorbed photon to the absorbing atom.)

its momentum must be c times hf/c^2, or hf/c. Since h and c are constants, always the same, the momentum of a photon must be proportional to its frequency. Double the frequency means double the momentum, and so on.

A photon thus behaves like a projectile. The atom which absorbs or "stops" a photon sustains a kick in the direction in which the photon was flying, like a man (Figure 7.1) who staggers backward when he catches a medicine ball. And, on the other hand, the atom which emits a photon recoils in the opposition direction like a gun that has fired a shell (Figure 7.2).

These are actual physical reactions occurring in the gains or losses of energy, when matter absorbs or emits radiation. These physical reactions have been proved by careful experiments. They have been verified, just as has Einstein's prediction that light, having mass, would be bent by the gravitational attraction of a massive body, such as the sun.

Today, scientists working on problems of future space travel point out that the ideal form of "jet propulsion" for a space

Figure 7.2 Atom man is driven back by recoil following emission of photon bullet. (Emission means that the momentum of the photon in one direction is balanced by the momentum of the emitting atom in the opposite direction.)

vehicle, once it was under way, would be a powerful beam of photons (light or invisible light), projected backward.

Such a jet would shoot out with a velocity of 3×10^{10} cm. per second, or 186,000 miles per second. It could thus, in time, increase the velocity of the space vehicle beyond anything that could be achieved by means of the liquid or solid fuels used in rocket motors at present. Something similar to lasers may someday be tried out as the generator for such propulsion by means of photons.

There is another important understanding that came largely from Einstein's great work in radiation problems. It is the complete correspondence between the energy changes in the absorbing or emitting atom, and the energy package or quantum carried by the photon that is absorbed or emitted, as the case may be. An atom that emits a photon loses just that one photon's worth of energy. An atom that absorbs a photon gains just that one photon's worth of energy.

Sometimes it is helpful to state this truth in the opposite way: When an atom loses a certain amount of energy through

75

Figure 7.3 Atom man on energy ladder. He can stand only at levels that his ladder allows. (Each level is represented by one rung, an energy level.) This is how things **are** in this quantum world.

emission, the resulting photon carries away just that same amount of energy. This means that the photon must have the energy size, or frequency, which matches the energy jump made by the atom which either (a) emits it, or (b) absorbs it.

An *emitting* atom makes a downward energy jump—from a state of more to a state of less energy. An *absorbing* atom makes an upward energy jump—from a state of less to a state of more energy.

Atoms will make only those jumps, upward or downward, that fit their possibilities or energy patterns. Each atom is like a man who can move up or down a ladder (Figure 7.3). He can stand only at the heights of the various rungs. He cannot stand at levels in between.

An atom is *not* like a man on an inclined plane or ramp (Figure 7.4) who can choose any level (of energy) he wishes, merely by going to the corresponding point on the slope.

76

Figure 7.4 Atom man on inclined plane. This is how things are **not** in this quantum world. This man could stand at any energy level he chose, between G, at the ground, and T at the top. He could thus rise by any amount between G and T or drop down by any amount between T and G. He would not be "quantized."

(We are using the word "atoms" here to stand also for molecules, which are the radiating units under many circumstances.)

Each atom, we see, is "quantized"—it has its own steplike pattern of possible energy states. It can absorb only photons of a size (frequency) that fits one of its possible energy jumps from one level to a higher one. It can emit only photons of a size (frequency) that fits one of its possible energy jumps, from one level to a lower one.

These statements are emphasized here because they are important ideas in the quantum theory of radiation on which are based masers, lasers, and so much else that occupies the attention of scientists today.

Atoms are somewhat like gambling machines, operated by coins. Some accept only nickels, some only dimes, some only quarters, and so forth. Those that take in (absorb) nickels pay out (emit) nickels. Those that take in dimes pay out in dimes, and so on. A typical atom might be represented by a machine which could accept (absorb) either nickels, dimes, or quarters, and might pay off (emit) in one or another or some combination of these particular coins (quanta)—*but* it could not accept (absorb) some intermediate amount, say 3¼ cents or 17 cents or 23½ cents.

(We are speaking here of atoms in the gaseous state, where they have greater freedom of action and can express their natural "energy preferences." In solids and liquids, the atomic and molecular crowding is great. These patterns are then usually blurred and distorted. The result is that an "excited" gas emits a line spectrum, while a hot solid or liquid emits a continuous spectrum.)

What equilibrium radiation means. When a body is in "thermal equilibrium," its temperature remains steady. So too does the power of its radiation at each frequency, or within each narrow range of frequencies, from one end of its spectrum to the other.

This means that if you say that one frequency represents the nickel (5-cent) size of energy, there will be as many of these 5-cent photons emitted as absorbed. There is a balance at the 5-cent level. At a level of double the frequency, the 10-cent photon size will also be in balance. Just as many will be emitted as absorbed, in any interval of time likely to interest us, so long as the equilibrium continues.

And so it will be for whatever frequency we may choose. Equilibrium radiation of a black body means balance between emissions and absorptions at each and every energy level. Each and every photon size remains in balance. Otherwise the temperature and radiation readings could not hold steady.

Before Einstein's paper of 1916–17 appeared, the leading atomic scientists, including Niels Bohr, had assumed that, just as there was one kind of absorption, there was also only one kind of emission. This kind we today call "spontaneous emission." It goes like this:

An atom becomes excited—that is, gains energy. Following the universal tendency of matter to move to states of lower energy, the atom will at some time emit that energy in the form of a photon.

Such an emission is a sort of private decision by the atom. It may happen sooner, it may happen later. There is an average time or "half-life" during which half of a great mass of such atoms will each have emitted a photon. We can measure this "half-life" period for a particular kind of atom excited to a particular energy level. Thus we can know how much total spontaneous radiation to expect within, say, the next one ten-millionth of a second. But we cannot know *when* a particular atom will emit. What is even more important here— in spontaneous emission, the moment at which atom A "decides" to emit has little or nothing to do with the time when its near neighbors, atoms B, C, D, E, F, etc., will emit. Each spontaneously emitting atom is "on its own." Only the *averages* remain steady for a large mass of such atoms.

Can a time so short as a ten-millionth or even a hundred-millionth of a second be worth mentioning?

Supposing we are considering spontaneous emission of yellow light, at a frequency of 5×10^{14} cps. We can see that within one one hundred-millionth of a second, which is $1/10^8$ seconds, there must be at least *5 million* completed waves emitted. That is the number of cycles which would go by between the instant that atom A emitted and the instant,

Albert Einstein

one hundred-millionth of a second later, that atom B emitted. We need not consider here how long a single process of emission takes. The important thing to note is that even though a large mass of atoms emit spontaneously within *a very short time,* it is not possible that their waves will be emitted "in step." They cannot be coordinated, either in direction or in phase. The result we have seen in Figure 4.3—a hash of radiations, bits and pieces, differing in frequencies, phase, and directions. In short, radiation that is quite incoherent.

Einstein's advance. Einstein found that there must be some sort of emission other than spontaneous. If one assumed that all emission was spontaneous, there was no way of accounting for observed facts of equilibrium radiation at various temperatures in the black-body cavity radiometer, such as we have described (Figure 5.1).

Something more was needed to reconcile what was known of the patterns of radiation and of heat motions in matter under radiation. What was missing was a source of additional emissions, a source which varied in response to the amount of radiation that poured in on the radiating matter.

Just this sort of variation was shown by the opposite process, absorption. Suppose you rained down *one* billion photons of a particular size on a mass of "unexcited" atoms that could absorb such photons. You would find in a certain time that a certain number of absorptions had taken place. Now if you rained down *two* billion photons on a like mass of matter, you could expect to find twice as many absorptions in the same time. And with *three* billion photons, three times as many absorptions. And so on, till the condition of saturation was approached.

This missing non-spontaneous emission must respond in a similar way to the intensity with which radiation rained down. Einstein found that at high temperatures spontaneous emission could account for only a small part of the total emissions that must take place in order to balance absorptions. There must be also a source of *non-spontaneous* emission.

Einstein found further that spontaneous emissions at any temperature could provide fewer of the low-frequency photons than of the high-frequency photons needed to provide balance at all the various frequencies.

Obviously this non-spontaneous emission, previously unsuspected and unidentified, must be especially active at lower frequencies and at higher over-all temperatures of matter.

Today this other kind of radiation, discovered, identified and described by Einstein, is known as "stimulated emission." Those two words provide the letters *se* in la*se*r and ma*se*r. Some writers refer to it as "induced" emission, others as "forced" emission. But all mean the same thing. And what they mean is truly remarkable, even today when it has been harnessed to man-made devices, such as the laser and maser.

Two possible interactions between radiation (photons) and matter (atoms) had been known before Einstein's revelation.

Situation One (Spontaneous emission). Excited atoms emit photons. Those atoms drop to lower energy levels—lose excitation. The photons carry off corresponding amounts of energy into the surrounding electromagnetic field.

Situation Two (Absorption). Photons of suitable size shower down on *unexcited* atoms. Absorptions result, through which photons disappear and atoms become excited, having gained corresponding amounts of energy. The probability of such absorptions can be indicated by a number, P. (For example: Under a photon shower of a certain intensity, the probability P may be 0.1—1 in 10—that an unexcited atom will absorb within one second. Then, among 10 trillion such atoms we would expect to find 1 trillion absorptions per second.)

Each absorption represents the disappearance of a photon and the transfer of a corresponding amount of energy from radiation to matter.

Einstein added a third situation, which no one before had seen:

Situation Three (Stimulated emission). Photons of suitable size shower down on *excited* atoms. Stimulated emissions result. Each is the emission by an atom of a photon of size identical to the stimulating photon. Both photons fly off together in the identical direction—the stimulating (first) photon, and the stimulated (second) photon.

The probability of such stimulated emission can be indicated by the same number, P. (For example: Under a photon shower of the same intensity as that in the example above, the probability will also be 0.1, or 1 in 10, that an excited atom will be stimulated to emit within one second. Then, among 10 trillion such atoms we should expect to find 1 trillion stimulated emissions per second.)

Each stimulated emission represents the appearance of one *additional* photon and the transfer of a corresponding amount of energy from matter to radiation.

Which will be most frequent—absorption or stimulated radiation? All these three processes go on side by side in the same body of matter under the influence of the same showers of radiating photons. Spontaneous emission remains, so to speak, unaffected by the presence of such radiation. Absorption and stimulated emission take place only with the help of such radiation.

Supposing that you threw a mass of coins into a crowd in such a way that there was one chance in twenty that a person in the crowd could catch one. A blond person would have the same chance as a brunet to catch a coin.

Would you expect that as many coins would be caught by blonds as by brunets?

Before you answer yes or no, ask yourself one added question: Suppose you know that there are twice as many blonds as brunets in this particular crowd?

At once you would realize that twice as many catches would be made by blonds as by brunets, simply because there are twice as many of the former as of the latter. Each person, regardless of hair color, has an equal chance of making a catch, but because there are twice as many of one hair color as the other, there should be twice as many catches by the majority group.

Now let us change the example just a little. Again money enters into the picture. You are going to play a sort of game with this crowd. This time we will use two groups called the *Haves* and the *Have-Nots,* or *Nots* for short. Each *Have* already holds a twenty-five-cent piece. Each *Not* has no coin. All *Haves* and *Nots* alike are seeking to catch another coin. You are going to throw out to them a mass of coins, so that each has an equal chance to catch one.

The rules of this game are simple but strange.

First Rule: When a *Not* catches a thrown coin, he keeps it, thus becoming a *Have.*

Second Rule: When a *Have* catches a coin, he gives back to you not only the coin he catches but *also* the one he had before. Thus he becomes a *Not.*

The first rule means absorption. The second rule means stimulated emission.

Now what will happen? Will you get back fewer coins than you throw out? Or just as many? Or more?

The answer, you can see, depends on how many *Haves* and how many *Nots* there are in the crowd. Each time a coin is caught (absorbed) by a *Not,* it is lost to you. Each time a coin is caught by a *Have,* it returns to you together with the coin he had previously held. A *Not* catch is a loss to you; a *Have* catch is a gain.

To assure yourself of a net gain, you must arrange that more *Haves* than *Nots* are in the crowd. Only in this way can you be sure of a greater income than outgo.

This money-throwing model represents familiar facts of the interactions of radiation with matter. The thrown coins are radiation-energy units, or photons. You, the coin thrower, represent the radiation field showering down photons on the atoms (players in the crowd). A *Have* player is an energized or excited atom, which has a unit of energy which it can emit when stimulated by receipt (catching) of another such unit (a coin you have thrown). A *Not* player is an unexcited atom. When he catches a coin (photon), he keeps (absorbs) it.

Players constantly change from *Haves* to *Nots* and back again as the game goes on. There is a circulation of coins (radiation units or photons). If you start with more *Nots* than *Haves,* your radiation of coins (photons) will be diminished (absorbed). It will enrich the players, which means add energy to matter. Only if you start with more *Haves* than *Nots* can you expect to get back more coins (photons) than you emit.

In other words, to get a net gain of energy by means of stimulated emission, you must first provide the right kind of atom population. You must make sure that the *Haves* outnumber the *Nots*. If you could get a large majority of *Haves,* or excited atoms, you could be sure that each emitted photon would come back amplified.

If, however, there are more *Nots* than *Haves,* you can be sure that emitted photons will be absorbed. Their number will be diminished.

This money-throwing model game has not mentioned one process—*spontaneous* emission. This could be included by adding a *Third Rule:* Any player holding a coin may voluntarily contribute it whenever he feels like it. Thus a *Have* may spontaneously become a *Not*.

We will not go into detail here with the results of such an addition. The model would still fit the main facts, but would not help much to understand what we need to know of the atomic processes of masers and lasers. Just one important point needs to be stressed: In *thermal equilibrium* the total number of *absorptions* is always balanced by the total of the TWO types of emission, *stimulated* and *spontaneous*.

Thus, we could say, in terms of our game, that when the catches by *Nots* (absorptions) equal the number of catches by *Haves* (stimulated emissions) plus the voluntary contributions by *Haves* (spontaneous emissions), then things will remain in balance. Radiation will not build up or diminish, and temperature in the radiated substance will remain steady.

However, if we wish to have an excess of emissions over absorptions, we must arrange somehow to make the population of *Haves* greater than that of *Nots*. This we cannot hope to do in a state of thermal equilibrium. We must find ways to shift or reverse the populations of *Have* atoms and *Not* atoms. This may not be easy, but we shall see that it can be done.

Why should we wish to perform such population shifts among atoms? Simply because in this way we can generate a large amount of *stimulated emission*. And *stimulated emission* has rare and precious qualities not found in spontaneous emission.

The existence of stimulated emission, unsuspected before Einstein, shows again how faithfully the human mind must follow the facts as they are observed, and how risky it is to rely blindly on the habits or prejudices we call "common sense." They must be constantly revised to match reality.

Picturing the three basic processes of radiation. Common sense might suggest that an *excited* atom would remain indifferent to the approach of a photon of suitable size, and do nothing that it would not do otherwise. However, if we refer back to the wave theory of radiation, we can find ways to picture the processes of radiation—including stimulated emission.

We might say that a man (atom) is likely to sing (emit) in unison or on pitch with another voice (the stimulating radiation) that he hears before he starts to sing.

A better analogy is the boy on the swing (Figure 7.5). Here (Figure 7.6) we see that he is pumping it up, higher and higher. The chemical energy stored in his body is converted by his muscles into work, the work he does on the swing. Energy passes from the boy to the swing as it oscillates ever higher.

Think of the boy as the radiation field, and the swing as an atom. Then his pumping up represents an *absorption.* Energy passes from the field in space to the atom. We see it is energy at a certain frequency—that of the swing's natural rate of oscillation.

Now (Figure 7.7) the boy has stopped pumping. He lets the swing die down in its own way. Gradually its oscillations diminish and it comes to a stop. This is like a *spontaneous emission.* The energy of the swing-atom is expended over a period of time.

Finally (Figure 7.8) we see something else. Again the swing is going high, but the boy has decided to halt it in a hurry. He pumps against it, reversing his former pumping-up actions. The result is that the swing dies down quickly.

This is like stimulated emission. The boy, carefully timing

Figure 7.5 Radiation boy and his atom-swing at rest. (No photons in sight.)

Figure 7.6 Radiation boy pumps up his atom-swing. (A photon is being absorbed.)

Figure 7.7 Radiation boy lets his atom-swing die down. (A photon is emitted spontaneously.)

Figure 7.8 Radiation boy pumps down his atom-swing. (Under the influence of a stimulating photon, a stimulated photon is emitted.)

his moves, has made the swing do work on him. The atom (swing), as a result, quickly lost energy to the radiation field (boy). This energy, emitted from atom to field, has kept strictly in step with the oscillations already present in the field.

In just that way, the frequency of a stimulated emission must always be the same as that of the stimulating emission. We may say, in quantum terms, that the stimulated photon is an exact match in energy content and in direction of motion to the stimulating photon. This uniformity is not accidental; it is basic.

One more comparison may make these radiation events clearer. Figure 7.9 is a handball player, just serving a ball. He has knocked it toward the wall just when he wanted to. Some of his muscular energy is shooting the ball toward the wall. This is like a *spontaneous* emission. Player = atom. Ball = photon.

In Figure 7.10 the handball player is catching a ball. He absorbs its energy with his hand and arm. The ball comes to

Figure 7.9

89

Figure 7.10

rest in his hand. It no longer flies through the air. This is like the process of *absorption*. The player caught the ball when it reached him. He could not have caught it a moment before or a moment later.

Finally (Figure 7.11) we see a player about to take a ball that has bounced toward him from the back wall of the court. He strikes it so that it flies forward with increased speed, sufficient to hit the front wall. To do this he must time the motion of his arm and hand exactly to the motion of the flying ball. Again the ball (photon) determines the timing.

Figure 7.11

P. A. M. Dirac

After he has hit it, the ball flies faster, with greater energy than it had before. This is like *stimulated emission*. Arriving energy, here represented by the arriving ball (the stimulating photon), has induced additional energy (the stimulated photon) to join it. The resulting energy is greater than that which triggered the action.

Spontaneous emission, we see, takes place for internal reasons. The atoms emitting spontaneously do so separately and

91

at random. We can predict, perhaps, how many of a trillion excited atoms will emit spontaneously within a millionth of a second. But we cannot predict which atoms will emit next. We know that the spontaneous photons will fly at random, in every direction. The atoms which emit them are constantly vibrating or dashing about. There is no agreement between them as to direction or timing of emission. Thus a spontaneous emission must be "incoherent."

Stimulated emission, on the other hand, takes place in response to the arrival of a photon of the same energy size as that which the atom is ready to emit. The timing is exact. The emission is "coherent" with the stimulating radiation.

The contribution of Dirac. Realization that stimulated emission must be coherent did not come at once. It was provided by the theoretical work of a British genius, P. A. M. Dirac of Cambridge University. Dirac's brilliant and difficult extensions of Einstein's ideas were made about ten years after the basic Einstein paper.

Before 1930, we may say, advanced quantum theory showed that stimulated emission must result in complete coherence between the stimulating and the stimulated photons.

This coherence covered every aspect of the electromagnetic waves. They must be coherent, or identical, as to

(*i*) direction, (*ii*) frequency, (*iii*) phase, (*iv*) polarization.

Coherence in phase means the stimulating and stimulated waves remain entirely in step. Coherence in polarization we shall not explain here.

Using quantum ideas, we say that there are two steps in every stimulated emission. First comes the "before" stage (Figure 7.12). Here a photon (P_1) approaches an excited atom. The atom's higher energy level is symbolized by its higher

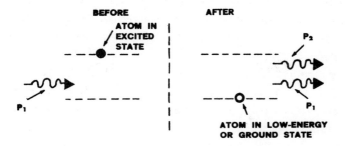

BEFORE   AFTER

ATOM IN
EXCITED
STATE

P_2

ATOM IN LOW-ENERGY
OR GROUND STATE

P_1

Figures 7.12 and 7.13 The two stages of the process of **stimulated emission.**
Before: A packet of radiant energy (a photon) P_1 approaches a suitable excited atom.
After: The atom has dropped to a lower energy level, and its lost energy now travels as an additional photon, P_2, in phase with the stimulating photon, P_1.
   WARNING! The use of **higher** and **lower** is only figurative, to indicate the change in energy. It does not mean that the atom is higher or lower **in space**, or that when it "falls" to the ground state, it actually drops like a lump of lead falling to the ground. The impinging photon reacts on the atom. The atom, in response, releases a like amount of energy in another photon.

position in the diagram. Next comes the "after" stage (Figure 7.13). An additional photon (P_2) has joined the first. Together they speed off at the velocity of light. The atom has dropped to a lower energy level. It is accordingly shown lower.

The atom may have dropped to its lowest possible energy level, known as its ground state. However, this is only one possibility.

We show the two photons separately. They are separate, in the quantum interpretation. Using the electromagnetic-

93

wave interpretation, we might say, however, that together they represent a single system of waves carrying double the energy of the system of waves that originally approached the atom (in Figure 7.12).

Here are the two stages in spontaneous emission. Before (Figure 7.14), there is an excited atom. After (Figure 7.15), the atom has dropped to the lower energy level and the photon it emitted is on its way. No other photon is involved. There has been no unison action or "cooperation" in radiation.

Finally, here are the two stages in absorption. Before (Figure 7.16), a photon approaches an atom in the lower energy state. After (Figure 7.17), there is no photon. Its energy has raised the atom to the higher energy level.

Scientists sometimes say that absorption is like the opposite of *stimulated* emission in this important respect—both take place in response to the arrival of outside energy (photons).

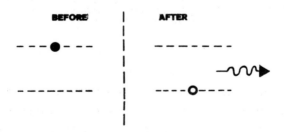

Figures 7.14 and 7.15 The two stages of the process of **spontaneous emission**.
Before: An atom is excited (has energy available for radiation).
After: The atom has dropped to a lower energy level and its lost energy travels off as a photon.

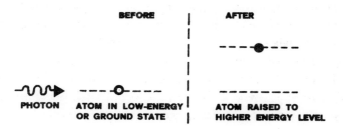

BEFORE | **AFTER**

PHOTON   ATOM IN LOW-ENERGY
OR GROUND STATE

ATOM RAISED TO
HIGHER ENERGY LEVEL

Figures 7.16 and 7.17 The two stages of the process of **absorption.**
Before: A packet of radiant energy (photon) approaches the unexcited atom.
After: Radiant energy is gone. The photon's energy has raised the atom to an excited level.

Neither is independent of the energy situation in the space around the atom. *Spontaneous* emission, however, depends only on the internal state of the excited atom and not on the energy situation in the field outside it.

The ladders of atomic energies—and their populations. Most atoms have many possible energy levels, ranging from the lowest possible (ground state) to states so packed with energy that the atom cannot hold any more and still remain an atom. (Beyond lie the states where electrons are lost to it— the states known as "ionization.")

Look at a body of matter composed only of atoms of one kind—that is, atoms of the same element. To simplify, we will suppose that each atom has four possible energy levels (Figure 7.18). They are labeled like floors in a building— G for ground level, F for first excited level, S for second excited level, and T for third or top excited level.

Each of the trillions of atoms in our sample must be at one or another of these levels. There are no in-betweens in this quantum world.

This body of matter, we know, is in a state of thermal equilibrium. That is, its temperature is steady. For our first test this temperature will be kept very cold. Now we take a census. We want to find out how many atoms are at each of the four possible energy levels. The number in each case is called the "population" at that level. We picture the size of each population by means of a bar on a chart such as census takers often use.

Figure 7.19 shows the result for the very cold body. By far the largest population is at the lowest possible level—the ground state. Each level above contains a smaller population. The differences in population size are very marked. Relatively few atoms are found in the most energetic population.

Suppose now that we expose the matter to increased showers

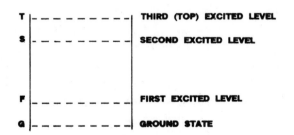

Figure 7.18 Energy-level diagram for an imaginary atom with four possible energy levels. The distance from one level to another is proportional to the energy, and frequency, of the photon which will be emitted, or absorbed, by a jump between those levels.

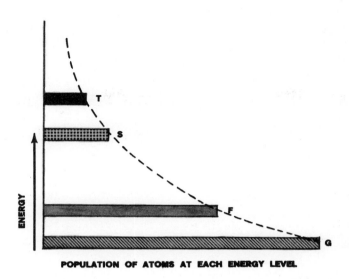

POPULATION OF ATOMS AT EACH ENERGY LEVEL

Figure 7.19 Populations at different energy levels in a body at low temperature. Differences in population size are emphasized. Here level F has about 72 per cent of the population of level G; S about 25 per cent of that of G; and T about 17 per cent of that of G.

of photons of sizes that these atoms can absorb. Finally it comes to thermal equilibrium again, its temperature higher but steady once more. Again we repeat our census count.

Figure 7.20 is the new population chart. The biggest population is still that at the lowest energy level, and so on. But the relative differences in populations are less. We see that population differences are decreased as temperature increases.

Finally, Figure 7.21 is a population chart for the body at an extremely high, steady temperature. Even here the populations at higher energy levels do not outnumber those at lower energy levels.

97

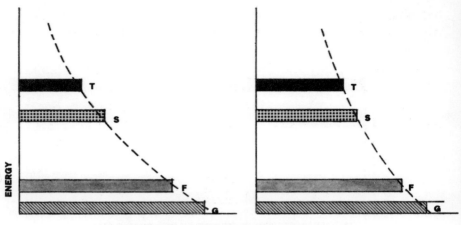

POPULATION OF ATOMS AT EACH ENERGY LEVEL

Figures 7.20 and 7.21 Populations at different energy levels in a body at a higher temperature. Differences in population size are now less marked. Here level F has about 85 per cent of the population of G; S about 42 per cent of that of G; and T about 31 per cent of that of G.

Populations at different energy levels in a body at still higher temperature. Differences in population sizes are still smaller now. Level F has about 88 per cent of the population of G; level S about 58 per cent of that of G; and level T about 48 per cent of that of G.

Yet population of a higher level **never** becomes larger than that of a lower level, so long as thermal equilibrium conditions continue.

Remember, as Einstein's rule of stimulated emission requires, increased radiation, which results from increased temperature, has a two-way effect:

(*i*) it makes more probable the absorption of photons by atoms at lower energy levels,

AND (*ii*) it makes more probable the stimulated emission of photons by atoms at higher energy levels.

There is no possibility that a body of matter in thermal

equilibrium will show larger populations in the higher than in the lower energy levels. In other words, no *population reversal*.

Yet just such a population reversal is required in order to make use of stimulated emission for the needs of man.

Suppose, for instance, that a way *could* be found to bring about such a population reversal. What if there were four times as many atoms in the population at level T as in that at level G?

Clearly, there would be a great chain reaction of emission—*stimulated* emission. Some atoms in the T population would spontaneously drop to the G level, emitting photons as they did so. Each such a photon would be *four times* as likely to cause the emission of an additional photon (by stimulated emission) as it would to be swallowed up in an absorption.

There would be a cascade, an instantaneous "landslide" of photons, most of them born of stimulated emissions, and consequently completely coherent and uniform with one another.

There would be, in other words, a *maser* situation.

But how could men manage to set up the necessary population reversals in the atomic world?

That is a question first seriously asked, and answered, a very few years ago, as we shall see.

8

THE FIRST MASERS

THE YEAR 1951 may stand as the birthday of the *idea* of the maser, as such.

Various scientists in the United States and elsewhere were thinking along similar lines, for important technical problems have a way of inspiring similar solutions in widely separated places—when science is permitted to develop freely, with interchange of information.

Nevertheless, the man with greatest claim to be called the originator of the maser is Dr. Charles H. Townes, who sat one spring morning in a park in Washington, D.C., thinking hard about very small things—microwaves.

Townes, then thirty-five, was a physics professor at Columbia University in New York City. He had been asked by the United States Navy to help find ways to extend to still higher frequencies the range of microwaves that could be used in communications work.

100

He was well aware that a limit seemed to have been reached in the march toward higher microwave frequencies. Tubes and resonant cavities could not be made small enough to fit these higher-frequency needs.

Well, then, if man-made structures would not do, why not try some of nature's smallest structures? Molecules, for instance?

Townes wondered, even more specifically: Could a great number of gas molecules be energized (excited), and then, in

Charles H. Townes explains the operation of an early maser.

response to weak electromagnetic waves of suitable frequency, be stimulated to emit additional radiation at the same frequency?

If they could, obviously amplification and oscillation would be possible. Amplification, because that is another name for the emission of *additional* radiation matching the stimulating radiation. Oscillation, because almost any device which is a good amplifier can be operated so as to stimulate itself and oscillate.

Similar ideas were in the minds of other physicists at about the same time. One was Joseph Weber of the University of Maryland. His paper entitled "The Possibility of Amplification of Microwaves by Systems Not in Equilibrium," a report on work done in 1951, was presented at an open meeting in 1952. When it was published in June, 1953, it was the first discussion along these lines to appear in a professional journal of general distribution.

Other pioneer thinkers in the maser direction were the Soviet scientists, V. A. Fabrikant, A. M. Prokhorov and N. G. Basov.

However, the title of "father" of the maser seems clearly to belong to Townes. In May, 1951, speaking on Townes' behalf, Arthur H. Nethercot advanced a proposal for a maser oscillator at a conference on submillimeter waves held at the University of Illinois. And on the last day of 1951 the outline for a gas-beam maser device was presented in the quarterly *Progress Report* of the Columbia Radiation Laboratory.

It was 1954 before such a device was finally constructed and operated. This first of all masers was the product of the teamed labors of Townes and two others—James P. Gordon, then a graduate student, and Herbert J. Zeiger, a research fellow at Columbia.

Joseph Weber

They cooperated too in naming their remarkable new child. The site of this informal ceremony was the cafeteria of Teachers' College of Columbia University. Coffee, rather than champagne, was the beverage at this christening, when from the phrase *Microwave Amplification by Stimulated Emission of Radiation* was formed the historic new word *maser*.

Maser number one. This first operating maser made use of a beam of ammonia molecules. Its very weak output of stimu-

103

lated radiation was at or near a single frequency—about 2.4 × 10^{10} cps, corresponding to a wave length of about 1.25 cm.

Its outward appearance was by no means exciting. Its operation was very limited. But it fulfilled the four basic needs that must be met in all maser and laser devices:

(1) *Excitation*—A method for exciting or energizing a sufficient number of molecules or atoms, thus preparing them for stimulated emission. Excitation is like cocking an air gun or winding up a spring. It stores energy where it can later be given off in a concentrated way.

(2) *Separation or Reversal of Populations*—A method for removing, or at least avoiding, the unexcited molecules or atoms, for these would absorb, rather than emit, radiations at the frequencies desired.

(3) *Stimulation and Amplification*—A method for stimulating the excited molecules or atoms to emit coherent radiation in a cavity or resonance chamber where such radiations can build up to usable strength. This calls for a suitable site or space for the chain reaction of stimulated emission.

(4) *Utilization*—A method for drawing off and putting to use the resulting coherent radiation.

Figure 8.1 is a simplified diagram of essential parts in these first masers. The process begins at left and proceeds toward the right, as follows:

(1) *Excitation*—A small furnace or heater (E) gives energy to molecules of ammonia, chemical formula NH_3. Ammonia molecules escape through H into a vacuum chamber. At this point some of the molecules are excited; others, however, are not.

(2) *Separation*—It happens, conveniently, that excited ammonia molecules are repelled by an electrical field which will

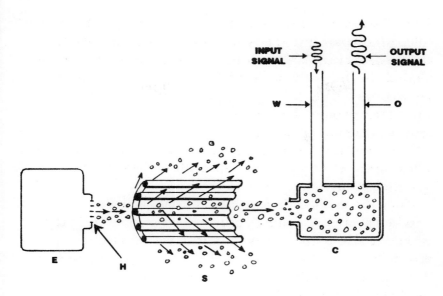

Figure 8.1 Essentials of a gas-beam maser.

E — Oven, supplying energy to many of the ammonia molecules. They stream out of the outlet, H.

S — Separator to expel less energetic molecules and retain the excited molecules on the central beam. (Shown as if cut in half.)

C — Resonant cavity in which excited molecules are stimulated to emit waves to which the cavity resonates (because of its carefully chosen dimensions).

W — Wave guide for input signals.

O — Wave guide for output oscillations.

attract ammonia molecules that are not excited. A separator (S) composed of charged metal bars draws out these unexcited molecules, but keeps the excited ones moving straight ahead. Because of this convenient way of eliminating the "Have-not" molecules and retaining the "Haves," such devices are sometimes known as *separation masers.*

105

(3) *Stimulation and Amplification*—The ammonia molecules which pass into the resonant cavity or chamber (C) are almost all excited. They constitute a reversed or inverted population. In the cavity some of them spontaneously emit photons at the 2.4×10^{10} cps frequency. These photons evoke still other photons by stimulated emission, and so on, in a chain reaction of radiation.

This radiation reflects back and forth inside the cavity, whose size has been chosen especially to reinforce waves of just this frequency.

Thus the gas-beam maser acts as a self-oscillator.

When it is used as an amplifier, the signal to be amplified is injected into the cavity in the form of electromagnetic waves that enter by means of the tube or wave guide (W). This radiation leads to even more rapid stimulated emission by the excited molecules.

(4) *Utilization*—The resulting coherent radiations are drawn off, as at O, to be "read."

Outgoing signals from such gas-beam masers are extremely weak, but they are amazingly pure and precise. Such masers are extremely selective as amplifiers. They will not amplify waves of incoming signals which are as little as 5000 cps away from their basic frequency of some 2.4×10^{10} cps. This means that they limit their amplification to a tiny sliver of band width.

A gas-beam maser in proper adjustment will deliver oscillations of such purity and coherence that they do not shift by more than one part in a billion or more, over long periods. Hence these early masers were commonly known as molecular or atomic "clocks."

An actual clock, regulated by such a maser, could be kept

accurate to within one second in a thousand years! A later form of gas-beam maser, using hydrogen rather than ammonia, is more accurate still.

No other device made by man has oscillated so uniformly and dependably. Whenever the utmost accuracy in timekeeping is required, masers such as these can supply the standards.

Gas molecules are not closely crowded together as are molecules in a solid. Thus the power output of such gas-beam masers remains low. They cannot be brought to the point of self-oscillation until a certain level of molecular "congestion" can be achieved in the resonant cavity. Even then the total output of radiation power is low. However, their other advantages compensate for these limitations, when the need is for a frequency standard or a super-accurate clock.

Newspaper and magazine stories today often sensationalize masers and lasers, giving the impression that they are all devices of terrible and destructive power—death rays, or worse.

The fact is, however, that the parent masers were mild and modest systems, producing waves that were weak but almost unbelievably pure, uniform, and coherent.

Weak as they were when measured in watts of power, they showed once and for all that stimulated emissions could be harnessed to work for humans. The ammonia-beam devices pointed the way to future developments almost beyond human imagining. Some of these we shall examine . . .

9

MASERS ATTAIN THE SOLID STATE

URGENTLY WANTED—
SOLID-STATE MASERS!

SUCH a sign, symbolically speaking, was displayed over the newly discovered land of masers. Molecules in a gas are "diluted." There are not enough of them in a given volume to supply desired intensities of coherent radiation.

But how, in the relatively rigid structure of solids, could the necessary separation or inversion of energy populations be managed?

Two basic methods have been developed by ingenious scientists. One we call here the *inversion* maser, the other the *multilevel* maser. Both use solid "active materials." Both operate at microwave levels and are aimed primarily at improving communications possibilities in these frequencies.

The inversion maser. Crystals are formed in fascinating and regular designs. Their molecules fall into the repeating patterns dictated by their internal forces. A stimulating discussion of crystal structures will be found in the book *Crystals* by Raymond A. Wohlrabe.

The compound which forms the crystal determines its structure or "lattice." This is the design of the crystal house. But atoms of other kinds may occupy certain sites or rooms in this house.

The crystal's basic compound is thus the "host." The minority or impurity atoms scattered throughout the lattice are the "guests."

Consider, for example, the well-known crystal known as the ruby. Here the host compound is aluminum oxide ($Al_2 O_3$). The guests in rubies are chromium atoms. They lodge in some of the locations which, without them, would be filled by atoms of aluminum. The greater the concentration of chromium atoms, the redder a ruby will look to the eye.

Forces within the over-all crystal lattice alter the behavior of these chromium "guest" atoms. Each atom behaves as if it were missing a couple of its outermost electrons. It acts, in other words, like an ion rather than like a complete atom.

When such chromium ions are placed in a suitable magnetic field, a curious thing happens. Former low-energy levels are split, in such a way that, by altering the strength of the magnetic field, we can alter the size of the energy jumps from one level to another. This means that we can "tune" the chromium ions magnetically to certain transition frequencies. Generally speaking, the stronger the magnetic fields, the higher the frequencies (in cps) involved in the transitions known as absorption and emission.

This is all part of a fascinating and intricate study known for short as EPR, meaning "electron paramagnetic resonance."

Relatively early in maser history, EPR methods were applied to make possible the *inversion masers.*

Let us take a simplified example. A ruby crystal will supply our "active material." It has been made for the job. It is a synthetic crystal, in which a small percentage of the aluminum atoms are replaced by chromium. There may be as few as one chromium atom to each 1000 aluminum atoms in the crystal lattice. Yet so tiny are atoms that even in a small ruby trillions of chromium atoms are ready to "perform."

The chromium has been kept "diluted" because for what is to follow, its atoms work better when they are separated, one from the other, by a fairly large number of the aluminum host atoms.

We begin by adjusting the magnetic field around the crystal to a strength which will assure a suitable energy gap, or difference, between a state of lower energy, which we will call "L," and a state of higher energy, called here "H." Many chromium atoms will then be found in the H energy state, but still more will be in the L energy state. (This is according to the rule we have already seen at work.)

Now we chill the crystal to extreme cold, using liquid helium or nitrogen to drain off the energy of random atomic motion which is known as heat. When the crystal is well chilled, the difference in populations will be far more marked. That is, far more chromium atoms will have lower, or L, energy than have higher, or H, energy.

(It almost seems as if we were working in the opposite direction to that in which our goal lies. But the great "switch" or reversal is yet to come.)

Now we apply to the crystal an electromagnetic radiation in the form of a microwave signal. Not just any microwave frequency, but a very special, shifting frequency. It starts just a little lower, in cps, than the frequency which corresponds to the energy difference between energy level L, below, and energy level H, above. (remember that for all radiation, energy is related to frequency by Planck's constant: $e = fh$, or energy equals frequency times Planck's constant.)

The signal generator is something like that used to transmit your favorite FM (frequency modulation) broadcasting programs. Its frequency can be continuously modulated—which means here raised or lowered. It is like one of those slide whistles whose pitch can be raised or lowered as you blow.

This radio-frequency radiation is rapidly modulated upward. Its frequency rises rapidly, like the note of a siren that is accelerating. Just as the frequency reaches and passes the frequency which matches the energy difference between the chromium atoms in the L condition and those in the H condition, something strange takes place.

It is, at that instant, as if the larger population of atoms in the L energy level had instantaneously been shifted to the H energy level; and the smaller population of atoms that had been in the H energy level, had at the same time been shifted to the L energy level.

We have somehow produced a larger population of atoms with higher energy than of atoms with lower energy. It is a "population reversal"—and such a reversal is the basis for maser action. Instantly, stimulated emission begins. Chromium atoms drop from the higher to the lower energy level, giving off radiation quanta or photons as they do so.

There is a mysterious-sounding technical name for this

trick. It is called by engineers "adiabatic fast-passage inversion." The inversion is, of course, the flip-flop effect that transforms a larger atom population at the lower energy level into a larger population at the higher energy level.

Does this seem like "something for nothing"? As if additional energy had strangely appeared from nowhere and been added to the myriads of chromium atoms, permitting them to give off stimulated emission? The true source of the additional energy is not hard to find. It is the energy injected or pumped in by the radio frequency signal as it slides swiftly upward in frequency.

Yet this does not remove all the mystery. To make this strange process clearer, let us use a simple analogy—and remember that analogies are only helpful comparisons. They do not *prove* anything. They merely help us to think more clearly about situations that otherwise might be confusing.

Here (Figure 9a) we see a man sitting, holding a stick on which a small weight can slide freely. The weight, naturally, rests at the bottom of the stick. It is as low as it can get. It cannot be made to do any work by sliding lower on the stick. (It is like the situation in which more chromium atoms are in the lower than in the higher energy state, and so unable to emit a burst of stimulated emissions, maser-style.)

However, we forgot to mention that this man is sitting in a speedy pursuit plane. The pilot of the plane suddenly does a half roll. The man now (Figure 9b) is suddenly sitting upside down, held safe by his seat belt. The weight on the stick is still at what used to be the "bottom" of the stick, but now that "bottom" is higher than the end which previously was on top.

What is the weight going to do? Clearly, it will slide toward

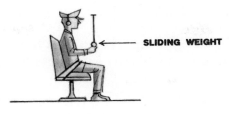

Figure 9-a

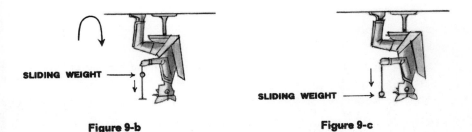

Figure 9-b   **Figure 9-c**

the earth—from the *former* bottom of the rod toward the *former* top. As it slides, it can be made to do work—that is, transfer energy—just as does the weight that drives a grandfather's clock (Figure 9c).

The sudden roll-over of the plane is like the reversal caused in the crystal by the rise in frequency of radio-frequency radiations as they pass the critical point. The subsequent "falling" of the weight and its output of energy are comparable to the maser action that bursts out so swiftly as the transition takes place.

Our analogy has been a crude one. Someday you may get a much more correct idea when you study the advanced physics that deals with what scientists call the "spin" of electrons. Electrons, like tops, have a sort of wobble or precession motion as

113

they spin. So too does this gigantic top, our earth. Its imaginary axis wanders about a bit. The fast-passage inversion involves the timing of the wobble or precession of the electrons as they spin, or seem to, in the magnetic field.

However, the subject of EPR could fill a book bigger than this one, and one far harder for most of us to comprehend!

One more comparison or analogy may help to make vivid the strange operation of the inversion masers. Imagine you

Nicolaas Bloembergen holds crystal which will be inserted into maser in background.

have a stadium filled with strong singers, trained and ready to sing a certain note—but only when they hear that note sung *to* them first. You stand among them blowing a sliding whistle, starting a little low, then swiftly raising the pitch. Just as you reach the selected frequency of sound, a mighty chorus roars out in one great burst.

It is that one same frequency, enormously amplified. It is, in fact, a sort of maser-style chorus. And in this same way operate the unexpected devices that are called "inversion masers."

Such inversion devices give maser action only in short bursts lasting a few millionths of a second. Bursts are followed by relatively long periods required once again to "pump" or energize the chromium atoms.

Microwave amplifiers operated by these and similar inversion methods have naturally suffered from many limitations. However, in 1956 a different and more flexible kind of solid-state maser was proposed. With it, continuous rather than intermittent action was achieved. It is—

The Multilevel Maser. A paper entitled simply "Proposal for a New Type Solid State Maser" first outlined this method. Its author was Nicolaas Bloembergen of Harvard University, who thus made a major contribution to maser "strategy."

In barely two years, practice once again realized what theory had pointed out as possible. A three-level maser was actually operated by a three-man team: George Feher, H. E. D. Scovil, and H. Seidel of the Bell Telephone Laboratories.

Their primary purpose at this stage was to establish that the bold Bloembergen proposal actually was workable. Other and better devices of this kind followed.

Here is a simplified picture of what takes place in such a

multilevel maser. We choose for simplicity a crystal containing as active material a group of atoms which have three energy levels, as shown in Figure 9-1. Three energy levels are marked—L being the lowest or ground state, M an in-between state, and H the highest of the three.

Next step: chill the crystal with liquid nitrogen or helium. This assures the largest possible differences in the sizes of the populations at different levels (Figure 9.2).

A "census" shows us, in fact, that the population at energy level M is only about 72 per cent of that at L, and at level H only about 17 per cent of that at L.

(Does it seem that we are moving in the wrong direction, making the ground-state population so much larger than the others? Wait and see.)

Now we saturate the crystal with radio waves at just the frequency which will raise atoms from the L state to the H energy level. (We take good care to avoid frequencies which might raise atoms from L to M!)

A point comes when the population of the H level is equal —or rather, almost equal—to that at the L level. This is what maser specialists mean by "saturation pumping."

Now see what has happened (Figure 9.3). The atom population remaining in the L level has become *smaller* than that in the M level, above it. In the diagram used here, there would be about 129 atoms at M energy for every 100 at the L level.

We have achieved a population reversal—a larger population at a higher energy level than at a lower. This is the necessary situation for a flood of stimulated emission as atoms drop from the higher to the lower level. Our convenient name for such a flood is, of course, "maser action."

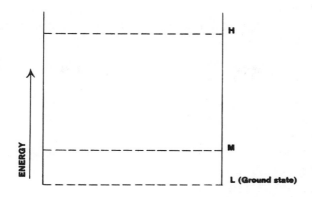

Figure 9.1 Energy levels of typical atom suited for use as active material in a multilevel maser.

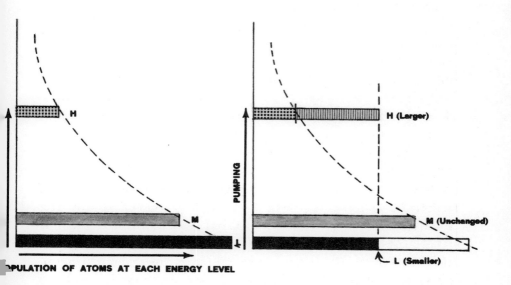

POPULATION OF ATOMS AT EACH ENERGY LEVEL

Figure 9.2 Energy populations in three-level crystal before start of saturation pumping.

Figure 9.3 Energy populations in three-level crystal after saturation pumping. Pumping frequency raises atoms from L to H. Now M population outnumbers the L population, and maser action can start, from M to L.

Here, maser action will emit the frequency which corresponds to the transition M to L. This is a smaller energy jump, hence a lower frequency, than that from L to H.

The pump frequency (L to H) accordingly is higher than the emission or masering frequency (M to L).

Again, by means of an atomic trick, we have managed to bring about a "maserable" inversion or upside-down population situation. This one is based on the fact that the chromium or other atoms used have more than two energy levels.

These energy levels can be shifted about, by means of the magnetic-field method already mentioned for the inversion masers. Maser makers must be scientists who know the propensities and energy preferences of available atoms under all sorts of conditions. For this reason maser work has been closely tied to, and has contributed much to, the vast and growing field known as "solid-state physics."

The three-level pumping scheme just described is by no means the only one that has been used. Some schemes make use of four, rather than three, energy levels in the same atoms. The basic principles, however, are alike. All manage to pump population out of a lower energy level until a higher energy level outnumbers it. The energy gap between these two levels must match the frequency at which maser action is desired. If the maser is being used as an amplifier rather than as a self-oscillator, this gap will have to be adjusted to the frequency of the signal to be received and amplified. Here is where the magnetic field of adjustable strength is such a help.

Picture of a Multilevel Maser. Figure 9.4 shows the principal parts of a multilevel maser. Heart of the device and site of the active atoms is a piece of crystal (C) enclosed in a resonant cavity or box (B) whose dimensions have been care-

118

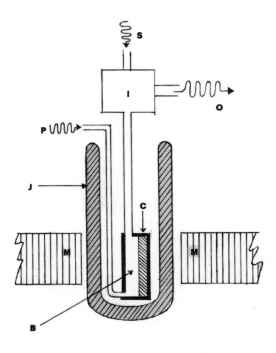

Figure 9.4 Multilevel masers have many parts.

fully chosen to reinforce the wave lengths at which masering is to take place.

The pumping energy enters via the wave guide (P) in the form of waves at a pumping frequency which here is higher than the amplified frequency.

The signal to be amplified is, in this arrangement, introduced by another wave-guide pipe (S), and the amplified signal is drawn off (at O) to be read.

The box marked I is a remarkable and almost incredible modern development called an "isolator." It regulates the

119

wave traffic in such a way that the weak signal waves will pass down and induce stimulated emission from the crystal, while the amplified waves from the crystal will be shunted off to O without harmful interactions.

The crystal and its surrounding cavity are kept not far above absolute zero temperature by means of the cold flask (J). Two poles of the magnet are indicated (M).

Various modifications have been made of this general plan. One of the most effective is known as a "traveling-wave maser." This does away with the need for a cavity whose dimensions must somehow be tuned both to the signal frequency to be amplified and the pump frequency used to inject energy.

In a traveling-wave maser device the crystal is placed along a wave-guide tube. Oscillations at the pump frequency are fed to it by means of this tube. So are the signals that are to be amplified.

At the other end the amplified signal is taken out. The tube is lined by a series of devices designed to make it a sort of double one-way street. An arrangement of comblike metal rods slows the incoming signal so that it remains in contact with the crystal far longer than it otherwise would. And another series of substances known as "ferrites" are so placed that they allow the amplified waves to move freely toward the exit, but weaken and discourage them from going in the opposite direction.

Ferrites, too, are products of the modern alchemical magic of solid-state physics. One can only wonder what James Clerk Maxwell, or Heinrich Hertz, or Guglielmo Marconi would have said to devices which operate in such improbable ways on electromagnetic waves.

Traveling-wave masers have shown steady and effective

operations in the microwave regions. They have already realized many of their designers' aims by amplifying very weak microwaves with the least possible "noise."

The benefits of cold. The low-noise operation of masers suits them especially to amplify very faint microwave signals with a "sky" background, such as those picked up from outer space by the receivers of radioastronomers, those caught from man-made satellites, and some of the signals of distant radar detection.

Never till masers were men able to amplify by means of devices maintained in extreme cold. All other common detecting and amplifying devices had built-in "thermal noise" because of the inevitable effects of heat motion in their resistors, their wires, and their tubes.

Since masers operate by means of cooperative action among atoms, they avoid the so-called "shot noise" which plagues all devices such as electron tubes, etc., based on beams and streams of electrons in space.

A relatively early and crude solid-state maser was installed under Dr. Townes' direction on the 50-foot radio telescope of the Naval Research Laboratory in Washington, D.C. There, safely jacketed in its ultracold "overcoat," it picked up microwave radiations from stars which scientists said were three times farther from earth than those which any other amplifier could have detected.

Still another maser achievement at that site was the measurement of infrared radiations from the giant planet Jupiter. Radiation from very cold and distant objects presents special problems in detection and measurement. Yet the results, when finally computed, enabled scientists to set Jupiter's surface temperature with some confidence at minus 150° C.

The great balloon satellite Echo I depended on a maser to amplify the signals bounced back to earth from its surface. That maser, installed by Bell Laboratories at Holmdel, New Jersey, responded to signals fainter than those that any other amplifier could have handled. Estimated power of the received signals was below one one-hundred-billionth of a watt. Yet the maser amplified these faint electromagnetic whispers until standard recording devices could convert them into permanent wriggles marked on paper. The success of the Echo I project rested on the unique ability of maser amplification.

Masers have unmatched possibilities, too, for responding to the faintest echos of radar. It has been estimated that a small receiving antenna plus maser amplification can get results equal to those of an antenna more than thirty thousand times its area which must feed its signal catch through ordinary microwave amplifiers.

The cold-jacketing of such masers is admittedly a nuisance. Handling liquid helium or nitrogen is often a balky as well as a bulky business. The tiny maser crystal must be surrounded by so much other equipment for supplying it with the right environment of temperature, magnetism, etc. However, in many instances these difficulties are well worth facing.

The low-noise qualities of maser amplifiers mean relatively little, however, when dealing with microwave signals picked up by an antenna which points toward the earth or objects on it. Earth temperatures, even in a Montana midwinter, are high enough so that much thermal noise is mixed into any microwave signals thus received. The extreme "noiselessness" of maser amplification would then be largely wasted, for the maser, like all faithful amplifiers, amplifies whatever it receives within its operating band width.

122

The noise that plagues communications receivers is so closely tied up with temperature that engineers commonly use temperature figures to measure such noise and its various sources.

For example, a fairly good non-maser amplifier of micro-waves may show a "noise temperature" of over 2000° Kelvin. Of this total the amplifier itself may well contribute 80 per cent or more, just from its own inner thermal agitation. The remainder can be traced to noise that has already been mixed into the input signal.

With a maser in good working order, however, the total noise level may register as low as 350° Kelvin, of which barely 1 per cent can be traced to the inner workings of the maser itself. The remainder is background noise that has come with the signal.

Robert W. DeGrassee, heading the team that handled maser reception of signals from Echo I, reported the following remarkable low-noise achievement: Total noise-temperature less than 19° K, of which about 13 per cent came from the sky itself, about 30 per cent from the aerial and input system, and the remainder—less than 11° K—from the maser device.

This was less than $\frac{1}{850}$ of the noise temperature that would have been added by a standard non-maser amplifier under comparable conditions.

The received wave length for Echo I was 5.3 cm. or approximately 5.7×10^9 cps. The faint signal received was amplified about 3000 times, which communications engineers will agree is "high gain." Yet maser magic kept the signals almost clear of the noise which otherwise would have swamped reception.

10

INTO LIGHT WITH LASERS

WITH the reality of maser action established so triumphantly for the microwave frequencies, scientists turned in the direction of a large step up the frequency ladder—to the levels of light itself.

"Infrared and Optical Masers" was the title of the paper, published in late 1958, which first pointed the way for this historic ascent. The authors were the father of masers, Charles H. Townes, plus another outstanding quantum physicist, Arthur L. Schawlow.

The two were, quite incidentally, brothers-in-law. They had worked together first at Columbia University where Schawlow was a postdoctoral fellow and research associate until, in 1951, he joined the Bell Telephone Laboratories.

This pioneer paper proposed that atoms of a metallic vapor such as sodium (Na) or potassium (K) might be pumped to excited states, then stimulated to emit coherent light radiations.

It also proposed a relatively simple but most ingenious answer to a difficult problem—the problem involved in what we called the third basic need of all maser operation: namely, a method and a site for the stimulation of the excited atoms. Obviously there was no practical way to design a resonant cavity which would have the width, length, or breadth of only a few light-wave lengths! (The wave lengths of light, we should remember, are about one ten-thousandth the wave lengths of the microwaves that we have been considering heretofore.)

Arthur L. Schawlow demonstrates a ruby optical maser.

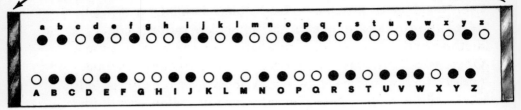

Figure 10.1 The shape of the laser is significant.

This supersimplified diagram symbolizes the many millions of active atoms by two rows of dots. The black dots show the excited atoms, in a majority after the pumping has added energy. The hollow dots are unexcited, or ground-state, atoms.

Laser action is ready to begin, for more atoms are in a state to emit than to absorb photons.

Note that the end at left is fully silvered, to reflect photons that fall on it. The right end is partially silvered, so that it reflects most, but passes through some, of the photons that fall on it.

Yet somehow a method had to be developed which would allow enough excited atoms to be stimulated at a time. Otherwise the total stimulated emission would be too faint to detect.

The solution proposed by Townes and Schawlow answered this need, and also the fourth need: namely, for a method of utilizing or drawing off the resulting coherent radiation.

Figure 10.1 is a simple diagram of their method. The active material is shaped into a cylinder with parallel transparent sides and reflectors at both ends. When emission begins (Figure 10.2), photons that do not travel parallel to the main axis will simply leave the tube through its transparent sides. If they do not leave immediately, they will do so after one or two off-angle reflections.

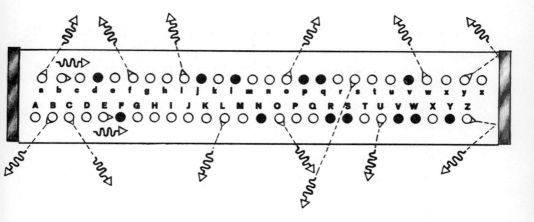

Figure 10.2 Emission begins within the laser....

Photons, which are emitted at an angle to the axis, pass out through the transparent walls and have no further contact with the active material inside. Thus in the top row the photons emitted from atoms a, f, i, o, s, w, and y are weeded out; and in the bottom row photons from atoms B, C, L, O, U, and Z.

However, photons emitted in directions parallel to the axis continue shooting through the active material, bouncing back and forth from the reflectors at the ends and gaining more photons through stimulated emission. Such are the photons emitted here by atom b in the upper row and E in the lower. See the next Figures for the results.

The only photons that continue bouncing back and forth through the active material are those that move strictly parallel to the axis (Figure 10.3). At each sweep through the active material, such photons should increase in number, thanks to the chain reaction of stimulated emission.

Thus the active material will be kept free of all but this growing group of coordinated photons, which remain strictly "on the beam," as pilots would say.

However, this growing radiation cannot be allowed to bounce back and forth ceaselessly between the two end reflectors. If one of these is made only partially reflecting—for instance, 90 per cent reflecting, 10 per cent transmitting or transparent—then some of the coherent light should emerge through that incomplete mirror (Figure 10.4).

The next year, in 1959, Schawlow published a suggestion that it should be possible to achieve such light-maser—or *laser* —action using a solid active material. He suggested for this purpose a ruby crystal—a dark-red ruby, for it seemed then that the processes for light might require the relatively greater concentration of guest chromium atoms found in the darker synthetic rubies.

The First Laser. By July of the following year, 1960, Schawlow's prediction was fulfilled in every essential respect. Only, the ruby color was paler.

Theodore H. Maiman was the scientist who first attained laser action. He did it using a small cylinder of pink synthetic ruby, about 0.5 centimeter in diameter and a few centimeters long. It was "pumped" by powerful bursts of light from a flash tube, similar to those used by photographers in their "strobe" lights.

This historic birth of lasering took place in the elegant modern building which housed the Hughes Aircraft Company Electronics Research Laboratory, nestled in the hills overlooking the well-known Malibu, California, beach where surf riders revel in waves of a very different sort.

Red was the color of the light that burst from Maiman's pioneer laser in Malibu. It proved to have a principal wave length of 6943 Å, equal to about 4.32×10^{14} cps. It was well within the visible spectrum. Thus visible light emission preceded infrared in the annals of the laser.

128

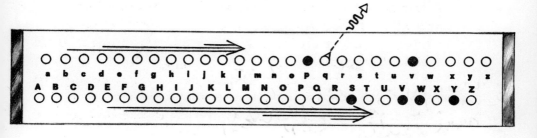

Figure 10.3 The build-up by stimulated emission begins....

In the upper row the photons emitted by atom b has stimulated emissions from atoms d and j (see top arrow with its triple shaft).

In the bottom row the photon from E has stimulated emissions from F, N, and R; while atom S is just being stimulated to emit also.

One photon from atom q is lost to the active material.

(The repeated bounces back and forth from the end mirrors are not diagramed here, to keep the pictures as simple as possible.)

The outcome of the stimulated emission is shown in the next Figure.

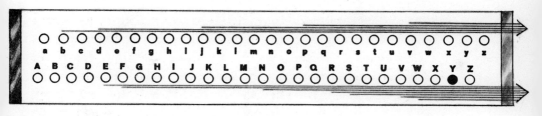

Figure 10.4 Grand Finale: The laser emits its coherent radiation....

Here the cascaded beams of coherent emission are shown emerging through the partially transparent mirror at right.

The upper beam has picked up additional photons from atoms p and v; the lower beam has gained photons from atoms S, V, and W.

Atom Y is shown still excited, to symbolize that most, but not all, excited atoms are probably discharged in the great laser bursts.

Now the de-excited active material in the laser must once again be energized, or pumped up, before the next laser burst can take place.

The duration of such a red laser flash was quite brief, perhaps 300 microseconds (millionths of a second). Yet obviously it was very intense. At its peak such a flash may reach a power level of 10,000 watts!

The light which emerged through the incompletely silvered end reflector was also highly directional. Such a beam commonly remains within 1/10 of a degree of the direction pointed by the axis of the crystal.

Also, spectral analysis shows that such laser beams remain concentrated within an extremely narrow band width. Their power "peaks" at, or very close to, the central frequency. They are in fact *highly coherent*—more coherent than any light ever before produced by man-made devices or received by them.

A few calculations showed that these little pale crystals of synthetic ruby were radiating, within this narrow band width, with an intensity equivalent to a temperature of 10^{12} degrees Kelvin. That is, a million times a million degrees of absolute temperature!

No wonder the ruby flash reported from Malibu became a signal heard round the world. Though red, it served as a great "GO!" signal. A historic rush of research followed—a chain reaction of experiment, study, speculation, and advance.

That reaction has continued since. The rate has not always been steady, but from time to time has been accelerated by great forward leaps. The race to laser with greater power and range still goes on. It continues even as these words are written.

More lasers. Within a few months many other laboratories had produced and studied laser action using rubies and .other crystalline substances.

By October, Robert J. Collins and others working at Bell

Theodore H. Maiman

Telephone Laboratories demonstrated the high degree of co-herence in such laser light. They masked all but two small holes at the emitting end of a laser crystal. The light came only from these separate outlets (Figure 10.5).

So completely in phase were these separated beams that they interfered with each other, producing the alternating

131

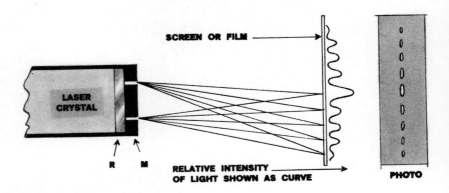

Figure 10.5 Crystal laser passes the acid test for full coherence. Light, emerging from **two different points** at the end of a ruby laser crystal, produced interference pattern in experiment performed at Bell Laboratories.

Emitting end of laser crystal shown at left, with its partially transmitting reflector, R, and a mask, M, with two separate slits to screen off all other emitted light. Rays of reinforcing light are indicated for lower half of screen. The resulting pattern is shown at right, marked "Photo."

pattern of light-and-dark patches which, as we have seen before, is the acid test for coherence.

These lasers operated without the aid of magnetic fields to adjust the energy levels in the chromium atoms. They thus used what laser specialists like to call "naturally occurring" energy levels.

What are the essential steps in laser action such as that first achieved by Maiman at Malibu?

The natural energy levels of the chromium ions scattered thinly through the ruby crystal look like this (Figure 10.6): G is the ground state. E and F are zones or belts of excited states to which these ions can be raised when they absorb light photons of various energies, some in the yellow, some in the green frequencies.

The discharge tube used to pump these ions is placed close to the crystals, sometimes wrapped about it in a spiral (Figure 10.7). Brief but powerful blasts of light from this tube flood the crystal with photons, including many that will excite the chromium ions as indicated (Figure 10.8).

They do not return to ground state, however, in a single

The "business elements" of a laser can be held in one hand. The slender cylindrical ruby crystal (darker rod) is clearly seen here, mounted in its reflecting case. Coherent light is emitted through the metal cone at right. Parallel to the crystal in this model runs the discharge tube (lighter rod below ruby crystal), which "pumps" the chromium ions in the crystal to excited energy levels.

Courtesy RAYTHEON COMPANY

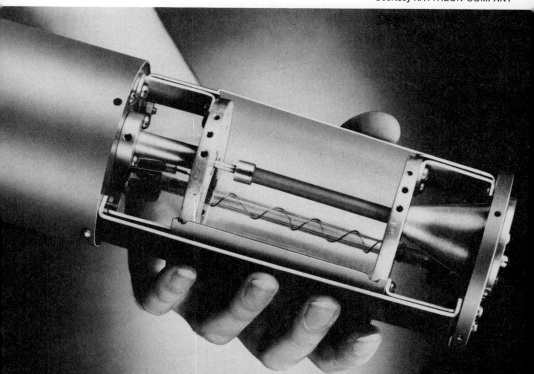

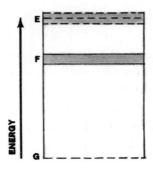

Figure 10.6 Energy levels of ruby crystal—first diagram.

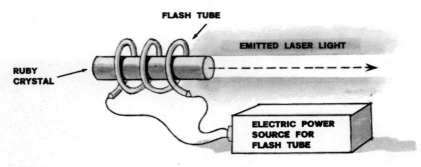

Figure 10.7 Essentials of a crystal laser, pumped by pulses of light from a photo discharge tube (coiled).

jump. They first make a shorter transition without radiation, down to one of a pair of energy levels marked M (Figure 10.9). This energy is passed to the crystal lattice as vibrations or heat in units called "phonons." It does not radiate in the form of photons.

134

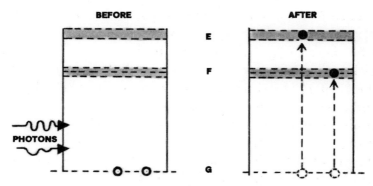

Figure 10.8 Light from flash lamp pumps chromium atoms from ground state G to excited levels in band E, or band F.

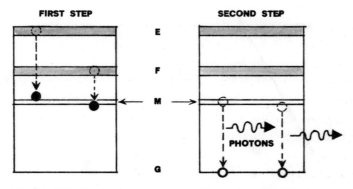

Figure 10.9 Excited chromium atoms lose energy in two-step process: First step: To metastable levels M. No emission takes place here. Second step: From M levels to ground state, with emission of photons by stimulated emission.

The chromium ions at the M levels are in what scientists call a "metastable state." The rate of spontaneous emission from these states is low. The average period of sojourn or residence in these states is accordingly rather long. The ions tend to linger in these energy levels.

The sheer pumping power of the flash tube thus accumulates larger populations in the M levels than remain behind at the G energy level. Here again we have the essential prelude to maser-laser action—a population reversal.

Some chromium ions spontaneously drop from M to G, emitting red photons as they do. These photons in some cases flash out of the sides of the crystal, but some move in the "right" direction—parallel to the axis.

We have seen already how these, bouncing back and forth in repeated reflections, build up into a mighty cascade which bursts out of the partly silvered mirror in the form of coherent, intense laser light.

Pulsed laser action. Extreme brevity and intensity are the marks of such laser bursts. High-speed cameras show that a crystal may emit in one area for a few millionths of a second, then in another area. Not only is the pumping power pulsed by the flash lamp, which does not operate continuously, but the laser action itself is even more intermittent and "spiky."

Yet the power attained during these tiny instants is enormous. It is the cooperative or unison power of millions of atoms working together, thanks to stimulated emission. As such, it is more intense, more united, and more uniform than anything produced when spontaneous emission dominates.

The off periods of pulsed lasers last far longer than do the bursts of emission. Even so, the problem of overheating has to be dealt with. Crystals are often liquid-cooled, lest they be distorted and perhaps even permanently damaged by the heat.

Pulsed lasers are also quite wasteful. Of the electric power that operates the flash pump, less than one hundredth of 1 per cent is represented by the power of emitted coherent light from the laser. Yet even this insignificant fraction is so concentrated in time, and can be so concentrated in space, that it becomes a tool of breath-taking power—both a promise and a menace for the future.

Powerful 50-joule laser beam instantly vaporizes metal, making hole in strip of steel, held in vise at right. The white hot metal and vapor can be seen clearly. A few inches away from this temperature hotter than the surface of the sun, the laser crystal itself is cooled to hundreds of degrees below room temperature. The cooling fluid circulates down through pipe at upper left, which is white with frost. Ends of 4 xenon flash tubes are seen. Scale is marked in inches at lower right.

Courtesy RAYTHEON COMPANY

Laser light as a tool. Laser light, we see, is almost unbelievably coherent in space and in time. Consequently it can be concentrated far more intensely than can any other light or radiation.

The results are awesome!

Crystal lasers, when actively pumped, radiate in short, powerful bursts. Thus their energy is already quite concentrated in time. Example: a modern high-power laser emits as much as 50 joules of light energy in a burst packed into a mere two-thousandth of a second.

The joule is a scientific measure of energy or work. It is the amount of work done during one second by a power of one watt. It happens also to be the amount of work required to raise a one-pound weight a little less than three fourths of a foot, or a weight of nearly twelve ounces by a full foot.

A ruby laser emits such 50-joule bursts at a frequency of about 4.3×10^{14} cps. Thus we know that each such burst must include about 2×10^{20} individual photons. That is, 200 *million million million* photons. (No use trying to picture to yourself just how many that is!)

Now, these vast armies of photons rush out within one little two thousandth of a second. Hence they are far more congested or densely packed than if they were emitted within a single second. Each such burst, while it lasts, attains an energy rate of 50×2000, or 100,000 joules per second. This is another way of saying 100,000 watts, or 100 kilowatts, of power.

This level of power would raise a 150-pound man 500 feet in one second, or 100 such men 5 feet. Obviously that is a powerful beam of red light, while it lasts!

This powerful beam emerges like a red pencil from the "business end" of the laser crystal. If left to itself, it marches

138

straight ahead, with almost no spread, at the speed of light. But it can be shaped and directed. It can be focused by means of a suitable lens or curved mirror. In fact, being so completely coherent, it can be focused into a spot unbelievably tiny—a spot which would make the area of a pinhead seem enormous.

Suppose we focus such a beam into an area less than one thousandth of a square centimeter. Result: the power density soars to 100 million watts per square centimeter during each laser burst.

The power does not increase, but its concentration in space does, and this is the principle of every cutting, piercing, and punching tool. Suppose you support a weight of ten pounds on a base ten inches square. The pressure at the base is a moderate one pound per square inch. Now if you reduce this base to an area of one thousandth of a square inch, the pressure jumps to 10,000 pounds or five tons, per square inch. At once things happen which could not have happened before.

This is what many ladies discovered when they stood with spiky high heels on asphalt pavement or soft earth. Their weight had not increased, but their penetration had increased alarmingly, because of the high pressure per square inch!

Laser-produced power intensities of 100 million watts or more per square centimeter far exceed anything that man ever attained before in sheer energy concentration.

Even sunlight can be focused to power densities not much more than 500 watts per square centimeter. This is enough to set fire to inflammable objects placed at the focus of a burning glass or mirror. It is enough to melt many substances. But it is very little compared with the energy concentration of focused laser light available now.

And within the next few years these attainable intensities

will certainly increase manyfold, as lasers become more powerful.

Sensational feats can be performed by such focused laser light. Among the many thus far demonstrated, are burning holes in diamonds, in hard alloy steels, and even in ceramic substances known for their high resistance to heat. The concentrated radiant energy swiftly vaporizes the material on which it falls. Within as little as one five thousandth of a second, temperatures as high as 10,000° Fahrenheit may be generated.

Laser light serves as speedy metal punch. Beam, coming down through tube, goes to work on a thin sheet of nickel. Note the spectacular "4th of July" display of molten and incandescent metal particles.

Courtesy TRION INSTRUMENTS, INC.

Metal vapor rising toward laser lens can be analyzed by spectroscope. This technique, known as "microspectroscopic analysis," is one of the many uses that lasers may have in industry and science. By laser-vaporizing even a very tiny sample, the composition of the whole mass can be accurately determined.

Heat builds up far faster than it can be conducted or radiated away. The matter simply changes state, becomes a vapor, and flies away in spectacular displays of white-hot and incandescent drops or particles, accompanied by smoke.

Even at relatively great distances, laser light can show tre-

141

mendous energy effects. It is estimated, for example, that a 50-joule laser beam at a distance as great as one mile could be focused sufficiently to char paper or scorch wood.

These demonstrations are unforgettable and often frightening. However, scientists and experts may be even more impressed by a demonstration of laser power which involved a far greater distance—from the earth to the moon and back again.

This was the moon shot performed first on May 9, 1962, between five minutes before and seven minutes after 9 P.M. During that brief, selected time, thirteen bursts of laser light were fired toward a chosen target in the dark part of the moon's face. . . .

And in due time—about two and one half seconds later—evidence came back to earth that the light had arrived and had been, in part, reflected back to earth again.

This was accomplished by a 50-joule ruby laser, product of the Raytheon Company, mounted on a telescope at the Lincoln Laboratory of the Massachusetts Institute of Technology at Lexington, Massachusetts.

Engineers from M.I.T.'s Institute for Electronics were in charge. They directed their shots toward a mountainous area of the moon, a little southeast of a crater named Albategnius.

So little spread took place in the beam that even at the moon's distance of 250,000 miles the rays fell within an area about two miles in diameter. Light from the most concentrated searchlight on earth would have spread to several times the moon's diameter, and been correspondingly diluted. Even the most powerful and precise radar transmitter could not have restricted its beam to anything like that little two-mile circle on the moon.

142

Professor Louis Smullin and Dr. Giorgio Fiocco of M.I.T., directors of the experiment, estimated that if a man had been standing near the center of the two-mile moon area, he would have seen each burst as a rather bright flash coming from that

The powerful laser that sent red light to the moon. Beam emerges from lens-like opening in center front. Xenon flash tubes project from four front corners of the large reflector box. These permit enormous power input, requiring heavy cooling. Refrigerant in reservoir box (on top of reflector box) is carried through pipe down to ruby crystal.

Courtesy RAYTHEON COMPANY

point on earth where Lexington, Massachusetts, is located.

No other light source on earth could have projected a similar intensity of illumination at the moon's distance.

Each of the thirteen flashes lasted only one two thousandth of a second. During that time about 2×10^{20} photons were launched toward the moon in a pencil about 143 miles long. Some were scattered and absorbed passing through the earth's atmosphere. Many were absorbed or scattered by reflection on the moon's surface.

Only a handful—possibly a dozen photons, in fact—made their way back to earth and down the tube of a 48-inch telescope at the Lincoln Laboratory, pointed to pick up just such reflections. They returned after having traveled half a million miles in about two and one half seconds.

A dozen photons of red light are far too few to be "seen" by a human eye, or even by a photographic plate. Their arrival was amplified by means of a photomultiplier tube and registered on an oscilloscope. Statistical methods were used to analyze the resulting oscilloscope patterns. The experimenters felt they had unquestionable evidence of the return of some of the photons that had been launched two and a half seconds before.

The team fired as fast as it could during the twelve minutes that the moon was in the favorable position. They were able to average about one burst per minute. Their maser had to be recharged, or rather repumped, after each burst.

All this was done with a single synthetic-ruby crystal less than one-half inch in diameter and six inches long. It was cooled with liquid nitrogen, for reasons which will become clearer in the chapter which follows.

It was pumped by means of a battery of four xenon flash

tubes, each pouring out pulses of 2000 joules energy lasting about one thousandth of a second.

Thus each energy input of about 8000 joules enabled the ruby to emit a burst of about 150 joules energy. About 98% of the input energy was lost—that is, it appeared as undesired heat rather than the desired coherent red light. Yet for the purpose intended, the moon shot experiment showed an amazing laser efficiency.

Blasting holes in diamonds and hard steel at near distances . . . shooting photons all the way to the moon and receiving them back again—such achievements have made men strongly aware of the laser as a tool to serve human wishes or dreams.

A common prediction has been that lasers will someday provide beams of energy by means of which satellites and space craft will receive power from sources on earth, even as they orbit about it or recede from it on their way into distant space. The men who work most closely with lasers hesitate to make such sweeping predictions. There are enormous obstacles to such energy transfers at distances so great as those indicated.

However, the laser leaders are certain that this new quantum device will excel in the field of communications and signaling. They see it, in fact, as the best available means for ultimately signaling from and to the moon and the planets of our solar system. No other device within man's reach today or within sight of man's ability can match the laser for such uses.

Dr. Charles H. Townes himself, the "father" of the maser, suggests that lasers may provide the means whereby humans on our planet seek to get—and perhaps even succeed in getting—readable signals indicating intelligent life on planets of suns *other than our own.*

Lasers would then become a supreme symbol of one of the most human things about human life—the insatiable and incessant urge to communicate, to send out questions and receive answers, to share knowledge and ideas with fellow creatures near and far.

(We dare not say "fellow humans," for the forms which rational and communicating life may take elsewhere in the universe may be forms far different from those we bear!)

Another and quite different possible use for lasers has also been indicated for the future. A tool such as the laser, which can almost instantly blast holes in diamonds, steel, and ceramic substances, can obviously also destroy men and the machines or weapons that men make.

A large part of current laser research and development is turned toward possible military uses in defense and destruction. The possibilities of thus using focused energy loom large today.

In the midst of sensational newspaper and magazine articles, predicting that lasers would become the legendary "death ray" that could annihilate anything, near or far, a small joke appeared during 1962:

Question: "What do you do with old razor blades at your house?"

Answer: "We vaporize them with a laser."

The men and women who work with pulsed lasers in laboratories wear heavy protective eyeshields and dark glasses. Permanent damage to the sight could be caused in a thousandth of a second. Laser light is no joke!

146

Courtesy TRION INSTRUMENTS, INC.

A relatively mild laser, with energy output of only 3 joules, cuts easily through a razor blade.

Yet laser light has been adapted to perform a most delicate bit of surgery on the human eye: the painless removal of a tumor from the retina. This was performed at the Columbia-Presbyterian Medical Center in New York City with a spe-

147

cially designed laser that could be aimed and focused accurately into the interior of the affected eye.

The time required for the actual laser flash was about one thousandth of a second. Yet it did the work.

In laboratory tests lasers have been used to "spot-weld" detached retinas in the eyes of rabbits.

All of these surprising surgical possibilities depend on the extreme power, coherence, and focus-ability of laser light.

Wherever in industry and technology the need exists for small spots of intensely concentrated energy, lasers are being tested and adapted. A thousand new possibilities appear— welding in cramped spaces and in vacuum conditions . . . cutting and shaping stubborn metals and ceramic substances . . . and even the selective stimulation and control of chemical processes.

Light and ultraviolet radiations have the power to initiate or hasten certain chemical reactions which would proceed sluggishly or not at all in the absence of suitable photons. With lasers extending their mastery into new frequency levels, the time may come when the industrial chemist will be able to pinpoint micro reactions with a precision today unattainable.

11

LATER LASERS—EXCITED STATE

AND CONTINUOUS

THE LAST MONTHS of 1960 and the first of 1961 brought a great burst of news of important progress in lasers.

From Peter P. Sorokin and M. J. Stevenson of IBM laboratories came word of a new kind of operation in which laser radiations left atoms still in a slightly excited state, as we shall shortly see. They used uranium ions as guests in a host crystal of calcium fluoride, and obtained infrared radiation at about 1.2×10^{14} cps, or 25,000 Å wave length.

Operation was at room temperature or lower.

The same team, during the first month of 1961, announced another excited-state laser, this time emitting visible red light at about 4.25×10^{14} cps, or 7,080 Å. Here the active material was samarium as guest in a host crystal of calcium fluoride. Operating temperature was very low—under 40° K.

One of the many wonders of lasers and masers is this spectacle of crystals chilled to hundreds of degrees below ordinary temperatures, yet emitting red light and infrared rays of the frequencies which for long were known as "radiant heat"!

The very next month, February, brought similar word from both ends of the nation—in California, Irwin Wieder and Lynn R. Sarles of the Varian Laboratories, and in the East, Schawlow and G. E. Devlin at Bell Laboratories, had achieved excited-state operations with ruby crystals. They used darker-red rubies—with chromium atoms replacing about one half of 1 per cent of the aluminum atoms in the "host" crystal.

With operating temperature of below 80° K they achieved two frequencies, somewhat lower than the frequencies of the first operational ruby laser.

Essentials of Excited-state Operation. The advantages of this new kind of laser operation become clear after we see what is different about its pattern of "pumping and jumping."

Here (Figure 11.1) we see in four parts what takes place in a typical excited-state laser using uranium as its active ion.

Pumping light at relatively high (green or blue) frequencies boosts ions from ground state to the uppermost energy state, T. From there they drop spontaneously to level S (2). This jump does not emit radiation. The energy loss is caused by cooling. The uranium ion transfers energy in the form of heat to the crystal lattice, and from there it is removed by cooling.

Next (3) comes the actual laser jump, from S to level F. Here stimulated emission launches a flood of photons of the infrared size.

But even now (4) the ion is not yet at ground state. It must make one more jump, without radiation, from F to G. This transfer of energy, too, is part of the cooling process.

Now what is the gain in this three-stage trip from T to G?

Mainly it is that the radiating jump ends on an excited

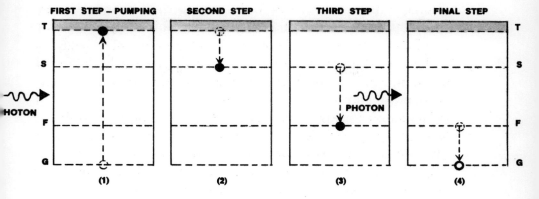

Figure 11.1 Four steps in the operation of a cooled laser, using the excited-state cycle.

(1) Photons of relatively high frequency (green or blue light) pump atoms from the ground state, G, to a top excited band, T.

(2) Atoms drop spontaneously from T to a lower energy level, S. This energy loss is accomplished by cooling, and does not cause the atom to emit radiation.

(3) Here radiation takes place—Atoms are stimulated to drop from level S to a lower level, F. This is the laser transition, and it leaves the atom with some energy—more than that at ground level. The atom finishes its radiation jump at an excited level: hence the name "excited-state operation" for this process.

(4) Now, by cooling again, the last extra energy is withdrawn from the atom. It falls to the ground state G, and is ready again to be pumped to T for another cycle.

level, not on the ground level. This means that cooling can constantly thin out the population at that level F, so that it never becomes congested.

In the first ruby lasers the radiation jump ended at the ground state, as we have seen. Hence the ground state became

151

quickly overcrowded. The only way to thin it was to work the powerful photo flash tube harder. This meant waste of power, overheating of the crystal, and general inefficiency.

The newer excited-state operation reduces greatly the drain on pump power, and brings the laser a large step nearer satisfactory operation.

Remember always that laser action can continue only so long as the population reversal or inversion persists. There must be more atoms at the higher than at the lower of the two energy levels involved in the jump that produces the laser radiation. When this population difference disappears, so does laser action.

Excited-state operation of lasers has not solved all the problems and difficulties that laser makers must wrestle with. However, it has helped, as indicated by a recent statement by Barton J. Howell and W. M. Macek, researchers into laser applications with the Sperry Gyroscope Company. They wrote:

> Until fairly recently it had not been possible to operate any of the solid-state [laser] devices on a continuous basis because of the heat effects caused by low pump efficiencies. The multilevel schemes that enable operations at reduced pumping levels did, however, show the most promise.

Such schemes, they conclude, "have been successfully used in continuous-wave solid-state lasers, both at room temperatures and at liquid-nitrogen temperatures."

The phrase "continuous wave" is the laser-makers' way of indicating steady rather than intermittent or pulsed emission. Often it is abbreviated as just the two letters CW.

152

For purposes of communications rather than drilling or cutting substances, CW operation offers clear advantages.

Before the end of 1962 many hundreds of laser devices had been tried, using a variety of active materials, various pumping frequencies, and other combinations of conditions. Continuous-wave operation had been achieved with chromium and samarium as active materials for the frequencies of visible light; and with neodymium and uranium as active materials for the frequencies of infrared radiations.

The samarium, it was found, required cooling far below room temperatures to obtain such operation with light, and the uranium also, to obtain such operation in the infrared. The chromium and neodymium could be operated continuously at room temperatures, however.

Other active ions which have lasered in the infrared region include dysprosium, holmium, praseodymium, and thulium. None of these, however, achieved the CW operation. Perhaps by the time this book is read such operation will be reported, for change and development are the outstanding characteristics of the entire laser field.

The list of laserable materials will certainly grow. One recent promising trend has been the use of special glass, rather than crystal structures, to serve as the host substance for the laser element. One such special glass uses guest ions of neodymium. Many other guests are under experiment and may soon be in use.

Glass has the advantage that it is an amorphous rather than a crystalline substance. Formation of special shapes is much easier in glass. Easier also is the obtaining of an even and consistent texture. Crystals, even when carefully made, have more tendency to develop flaws and trouble spots which show

153

up when they become heated from pumping. Some plastic substances and even certain liquids have also been shown to possess the characteristics required for laser action.

A great variety of possible improvements in the pumping process itself have been proposed and are being tested. Experts say that it should not be necessary always to pump by means of the power-consuming and heat-generating flash tubes.

Light from other and "milder" sources can be focused on a laser crystal or glass rods by means of curved mirrors or lenses. The source should be rich in green and blue frequencies suited to the pumping of the active ions being used. One group of proposals which attracts much interest calls for the focusing of sunlight on laser crystals or glass laser rods. This opens the possibility for a type of pumping such as might be used to energize lasers carried by satellites or space vehicles. It would eliminate the need for the bulky and heavy power sources required to fire the flash lamps.

Another line of investigation is that of laser amplifiers. This consists basically of using lasers "in tandem," one after another. Laser A emits a less powerful beam, which stimulates identical frequency emissions from Laser B, the amplifier.

For example, a recent announcement told of a tandem arrangement in which the A laser was pumped at about 250 joules, while the B or amplifier laser was pumped at about eight times that energy, or 2000 joules. The result was that the output energy from A was increased as much as 700 times, thanks to the B amplification.

The output of a lower-power laser is more easily controllable. It is suited for "modulation," the process which impresses signals, information, and messages on the emitted waves. The amplification can then build up the modulated waves to the desired energies. Such at least is the theory, which

154

is similar to that which has been followed with success in the design of radio transmitters and receivers.

Wherever one turns in the seething, expanding world of lasers, new ideas are being broached, discussed, tried out. A dozen are dropped, but one survives to be developed further. No one today can predict with confidence the direction that technical advance will take within a few years. Certain appears to be one thing only: lasers are here to stay, in whatever form, and will profoundly influence human life.

At the present time there is only one form of laser which is continuous in the full sense of the word—that is, it emits radiation whose frequency remains uniform, predictable, and dependable over long periods of time. This laser form has not yet been described in this book. It is neither so spectacular nor so powerful as the solid-state devices we have reviewed so far. However, in the details of its "inner workings" it is in many ways more remarkable and more "improbable" than they are.

It is the *gas laser,* which we shall call here—

The truly continuous laser. During September 1959, under the chairmanship of Dr. Townes, a conference was held in New York on quantum electronics and related subjects. At that time a paper was presented by Ali Javan of Bell Laboratories. Its title was one of those fascinating ones that seem to abound in laser literature: "Possibilities of Obtaining Negative Temperature in Atoms by Electron Impact."

Basically it proposed an ingenious strategy for exciting atoms, for reversing or inverting populations (which is the meaning of "negative temperature"), and for achieving laser action.

By early 1961 Javan and his associates, William R. Bennett, Jr., and Donald R. Herriott, were able to report successful operation of such a device. That report was called "Population Inversion and Continuous Optical Maser Oscillations." An optical maser is, of course, just another name for a laser.

Thus was born the gas laser, whose secrets we shall now seek to probe.

Gas lasers function quite differently from the pulsed solid-state lasers. Gas lasers are not powerful. Their steady laser beams will not burn holes in diamonds or vaporize steel sheets. They hold no apparent possibilities of being developed into generators of "death rays."

However, they emit light and infrared radiation that is in every way more uniform than that of the solid-state lasers so far described. Gas-laser light is the ultimate in coherence and uniformity. It is emitted in band widths so narrow as to seem almost unbelievable. It opens new fields for experiments, standardizations, and demonstrations that depend on the utmost in controlled accuracy of radiation.

Beams from such devices can interact to produce interference effects which scientists find extraordinary. Experiments in fact show that laser beams can be made to exhibit the effect known in acoustics as "beats." These are related to the difference and, likewise, to the sum of the frequencies of two beams that are mixed together.

Harmonics have also been observed in laser light. A harmonic is an exact multiple of the fundamental frequency. Thus a guitar string tuned to 1000 cps would have harmonics at 2000, 3000, 4000 cps, etc. And an intensely focussed beam of laser light at a frequency of 4.3×10^{14} cps (red) may be made to show some radiation at 8.6×10^{14} cps (ultraviolet). This is known commonly as "frequency doubling" and is something quite new, so far as light is concerned.

Never before have scientists been able to work with light

coherent enough to exhibit these effects. The possibility appears, in fact, that these laboratory achievements may be used in communications systems that employ carrier waves at infra-red and light frequencies.

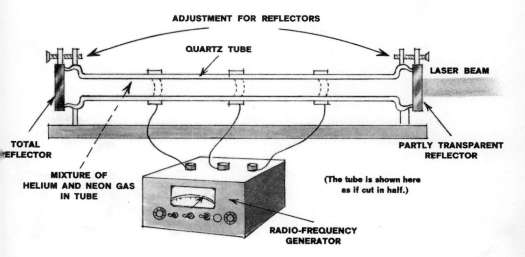

Figure 11.2 A gas laser is shaped like a "magic wand":
Far longer than a typical crystal in a solid-state laser, the quartz tube of a gas laser has the same functions: (a) to hold the active material, (b) to release off-angle radiation through its transparent sides, (c) to provide maximum stimulated emission as the on-axis radiation surges back and forth along its length.
The laser beam emitted through the partly transparent reflector (right) is highly coherent and highly parallel. Its spread may be less than 1/60 of a degree. No light source but a laser emits a beam so nearly parallel.

Gas lasers are put together in a manner that seems strange until one understands the distinctive way they work. Here is a simplified diagram of such a laser (Figure 11.2).

A long, narrow quartz tube contains a gas mixture, commonly composed of a majority of helium and a minority of neon atoms. At each end of the tube is a reflector. One or both of these are partly transparent. This permits the coherent light to "leak out" when lasering is well under way.

Several metal bands around the tube are connected to a radio-frequency generator, G. It works somewhat like a small broadcasting station, and pours its electromagnetic energy into the tube. This is the "pumping" energy that raises the gas molecules to levels from which they will fall, radiating as they do so.

The actual power required for a typical gas laser of laboratory size is small—as little as 40 watts may do. That is no more than the power consumed by a moderate-size electric light bulb.

This power pumps or energizes the gas atoms at a radio frequency—perhaps about 4×10^7 cps—but the emitted laser radiation has a frequency many million times as high! A typical gas laser sold commercially will emit either in the infrared at about 2.6×10^{14} cps or in the visible red at about 4.7×10^{14} cps.

This is quite different from all masers and lasers we have seen so far in this book. All the others use pump power supplied at frequencies *higher* than the frequency of the emitted vibrations.

These other masers and lasers are like gambling machines that receive fifty-cent pieces but pay off in smaller coin, such as twenty-five-cent pieces. The photons that supply them with energy are bigger energy units than the photons they emit.

The gas laser, however, is like a strange sort of gambling machine which receives pennies, but whose pay-off is in super-coins, or possibly jewels, worth $100,000 each.

In all these cases, however, the total value (energy) of the input is far larger than the total value (energy) of the output.

158

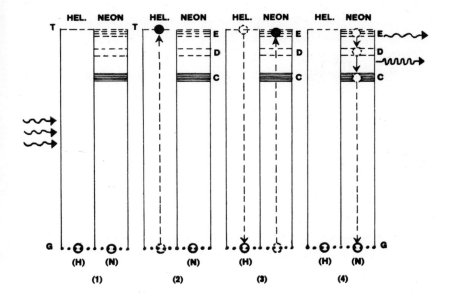

Figure 11.3 Strange strategy of "pumping and jumping" in the gas laser.
(1) Radio-frequency waves (indicated at left) surge through a mixture of helium and neon gas, both shown at ground state G.
(2) Helium atoms are excited to large energy jump to level T, which is at same energy level as band E for neon.
(3) In collisions, helium atoms shift energy to neon atoms. Helium atoms drop back to ground state G, while neon atoms are raised to excited level E.
(4) Neon atoms drop, in three jumps:
   (a) E to D, which emits photons in infrared.
   (b) D to C, which emits photons in visible red.
   (c) Final jump, C to G, which does not emit radiation.
   Atoms are again ready for excitation.

By suitable adjustments, the gas laser may "favor" either the E to D (infrared) or the D to C (visible red) jumps, and emit its laser radiation at either frequency.

Less than one ten-thousandth of the electric power consumed by a typical gas laser is represented by the power of the coherent radiation that it emits. Its efficiency is low.

Patterns of energy exchange. What goes on inside a gas laser as it operates continuously is a strange story of atomic "strategy." The pattern of its energy exchanges could hardly have seemed possible to scientists a few decades ago.

The "injected" radio-frequency waves excite the atoms of gas inside the quartz tube. Many of the helium atoms make a large energy jump (Figure 11.3) from the ground state G to a level marked T. This represents an energy gain of nearly 20 electron volts. However, it is not the helium atoms which emit the laser light.

The developers of this method knew that neon atoms have a number of energy levels, marked E, at just about the same energy level as T. They knew also that colliding atoms commonly transfer "chunks" of energy from one to the other, without radiating away bits of that energy.

There is in fact an intriguing scientific name for such complete energy transfers by means of collisions. They are called "collisions of the second sort." In such a collision—as shown here—the helium atom loses all its energy and returns to the ground state. The neon atom now has nearly 20 electron volts of energy. It is the neon atom which will now emit.

There are more neon atoms in the E band than in another band of energy levels below, marked D. Collisions with helium atoms have not raised neon atoms to the D levels, because those are too far below the helium's T level.

We have, then, a population reversal, and the stage is set for laser action as neon atoms are stimulated to drop from E-to-D levels, emitting coherent photons as they do.

160

Once at D energy levels, the neon atoms are ready for the next jump, to one of several C levels. The D-to-C jump is about double that from E to D.

Laser action is possible also at this D to C transition. Suitable adjustment of the distance between the end mirrors and other operating conditions of the gas laser can, in fact, "tune" it to emit mainly either at the D-to-C or at the E-to-D frequency.

If the lasering is arranged to take place at the smaller E-to-D jump, the principal emitted frequency will be in the infrared, at about 2.6×10^{14} cps. If, however, the adjustments provide laser "resonance" for the D-to-C jump, then the principal emitted frequency will be in the visible red, at about 4.7×10^{14} cps.

Because these levels—E, D, and C—are all multiple, there are various frequency choices which may be made. The distance apart and exact angle of the two reflectors are critical. Even tiny adjustments will influence greatly the pattern of laser emission.

The quartz tube, though it is millions of times as long as the tiny wave lengths of laser light that come out of it, is really one great resonant cavity. For this reason the end-mirror mountings are often made of a metal called "invar," which has practically no expansion when heated. Its length remains almost invariable. Hence it helps keep the exact spacing desired for resonance in the tube, even though it grows warmer as the radio-frequency pumping action proceeds.

In the solid-state lasers, whether they use crystals or glass cylinders to provide the active ions, those small cylinders themselves serve as the resonant cavities. Hence these cylinders must be shaped with the utmost precision, and they must be guarded as much as possible against distorting effects of heat.

If excessive heat builds up within a solid-state laser, the situation is almost as if a violin, while being played, became distorted by heat into the shape of a viola or small cello. The effects on its tone—and on the frequencies of the sounds it emits—could be imagined!

Because of the moderate and steady pumping power used with gas lasers, they have less trouble of this kind. They can be operated continuously and though their laser beams are feeble, they are steady and dependable.

Quite likely you may someday have the opportunity to see gas lasers in action in some school or university laboratory. Whether they make use of the helium-neon gas combination or some other kind of gaseous active material, they will probably be based on the same general patterns of "pumping and jumping" as those which have been illustrated here.

Masers and lasers are tools. The best tool is the one that best fits the particular job you want to do with it. Sometimes you may want a sledge hammer (or a powerfully pulsed solid-state laser). Sometimes you may want a tiny tack hammer (or a gas laser).

Big or little, hammers are based on the same principles of energy accumulation and energy delivery to the object struck. Powerful and spasmodic or weak and steady, lasers are based on the same fundamental principles of population reversal followed by stimulated emission.

The applications differ; the underlying principles remain the same.

However, something still more unusual is yet to come—the "injection" laser.

12

INTRODUCING THE INJECTION

LASER

A JULY date once again looms large in laser history. This was July 9, 1962—barely two years after the first red flash from Maiman's number-one laser in Malibu.

The new revelation came from the other side of the United States. From Lincoln Laboratories of the Massachusetts Institute of Technology, Robert J. Keyes and Theodore M. Quist revealed that they had caused a semiconductor diode to emit infrared radiations.

This was not yet a laser. These radiations had lacked the coherence, the intensity, and the concentration that meant maser action. Yet a new and exciting possibility was revealed.

Research projects were launched in a hurry. Interest and anticipation arose. The race toward a direct-conversion or injection laser was under way.

Keyes and Quist had "injected" or driven a powerful electric current into a diode formed from a crystal of gallium

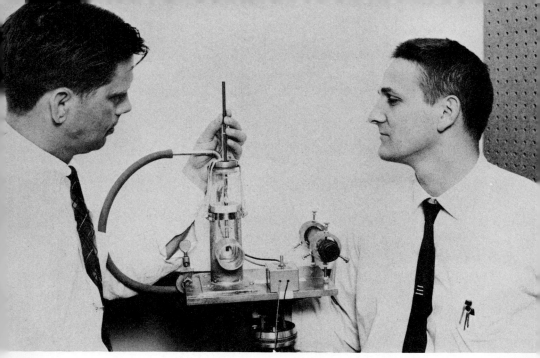

Courtesy M.I.T. LINCOLN LABORATORY

R J. Keyes, left, and T. M. Quist of M.I.T. Lincoln Laboratory examine assembly which holds gallium arsenide diode that will transmit twenty television channels or 20,000 voice channels on a single beam of intense infrared light. Diode may be seen in the circular window at bottom end of vertical black rod inside glass container; small telescope for aiming the light beam is at the right.

arsenide (GaAs) into which tiny but precise amounts of two "impurities" had been mixed during its formation. (It was, of course, synthetically made.)

The result of these electric-current injections had been infrared radiation at a frequency of about 3.5×10^{14} cps, the wave length being near 8400 Å. How could a diode do this?

Data on diodes. A diode is one of those rather improbable solid-state devices which belong to the transitor family. Actually it would be closer to fact to say that a transistor is a sort of combination or fusion of two diodes. Here we shall be able to offer only a sketchy picture of how a diode operates.

Diode action takes place within a crystalline solid. It contains certain impurities which either add or remove electrons from some points in the crystal lattice. These electron excesses and deficiencies are able to wander about within the crystal at certain energy levels. Not, however, at *any* or *all* energy levels—only at *certain* energy levels, for these energy possibilities, too, are "quantized."

Part of a diode is doped with impurities which set free excess electrons. This is called the *n* region, for electrons are negative charges. Another part of the same diode is doped with impurities which remove or withhold electrons. The holes where these electrons should have been act like positive charges. These holes are able to wander about also, and to respond to electric forces. The part where these holes have the "upper hand" is known as the *p* region, for positive.

Between the *n* and *p* regions is an important junction area which is the heart of diode action.

Here (Figure 12.1) is a simplified diode, showing the *n*, the *p*, and the junction regions.

Keyes and Quist had injected a strong stream of electrons— another name for an electric current—into the *n* region. The circuit was completed by withdrawing electrons from the *p* region. The result was: at the junction, sharp energy drops took place. Electrons dropped—in energy, not in position, of course—from a level known as the "conduction-energy band" to a lower level known as the "valence-bond energy band."

The energy lost by these electrons appeared as radiation. The size of the energy drop corresponded to the observed frequency of that radiation.

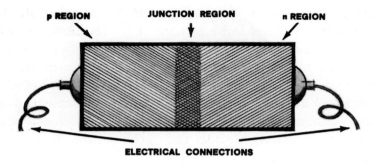

ELECTRICAL CONNECTIONS

Figure 12.1 Diagram of a diode.

A single semiconductor crystal. (It may also be formed as a sandwich of separate pieces). Systemic "doping" or introduction of "impurities" has created two major zones and between them a sort of no-man's land or transition region...

In the **n** region impurities release electrons (negative charges) that wander about the crystal lattice at certain energy levels.

In the **p** region other impurities remove electrons, leaving "holes" that act like positive charges. These holes wander about the crystal lattice at certain energy levels, differing from those of the electrons mentioned above.

The junction region is the heart of diode action. Here the impurities balance or counteract each other, wandering electrons and holes are scarcest, and the basic diode processes take place.

This process was a historic "first." It was a *direct conversion* of electric current into radiation. There had been no preliminary heating of a mass of matter, as in flame or electric lights. The diode radiations took place in crystalline material cooled to a point near absolute zero. Allowing it to become warmer would hinder, not help, the radiative process.

Semiconductor diodes were well known as sensitive detectors of infrared and light radiations. These important applications depend on what scientists called *the photoconductive effect* and on a related behavior called the *photovoltaic effect.*

166

These effects make possible, for example, the use of such semiconductors in the solar cells which provide some satellites with power direct from the sun's rays.

With the help of these important effects, radiations of light or radiant heat falling on semiconductor diodes are converted directly into electric currents. Now Keyes and Quist had accomplished the reverse: they had used the diode to convert electric current directly into radiation. We might even say that the injection laser makes use of

the *inverse* photoconductive effect

OR the *inverse* photovoltaic effect.

(Though naming a new process does not explain it, still an accurate label is a source of comfort until explanation can follow.)

Enlarged view of tiny gallium arsenide diode that will transmit twenty television pictures simultaneously on a single beam of intense infrared light. The diode is just in back of the small hole in the center, through which the infrared light beam is emitted.

Courtesy M.I.T. LINCOLN LABORATORY

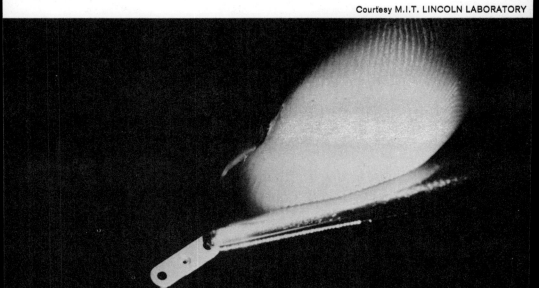

With this great breakthrough at Lincoln Laboratories came new and urgent questions:

Could a semiconductor diode, radiating in this way, be induced or stimulated to laser action also?
Could coherent as well as spontaneous (incoherent) radiations be emitted in the process of direct conversion of electric current into the vibrations of invisible light?

The answer appeared very soon—in fact, by November 1, 1962. It was not only *yes,* but a three-fold YES!!!

Research team at work on injection laser. General Electric Research Laboratory's scientists, left to right, Richard O. Carlson, Theodore J. Soltys, Robert N. Hall, Jack D. Kingsley and Gunther Fenner.

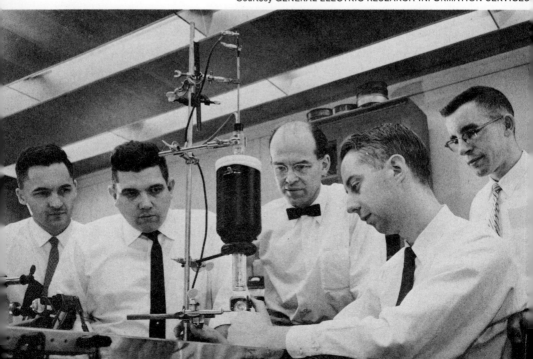

Each exclamation point symbolizes a separate, independent confirmation by a different scientific team, working in a different laboratory.

The race to be first to report this *Yes* was dramatic. It became one of the great "chase" sequences of modern technology. The results of the first two teams to cross the public finish line were actually published on the same date—November 1—in two journals of the American Institute of Physics.

The *Physical Review Letters* of that date printed a short paper signed by five scientists of the General Electric Research Laboratory of Schenectady, New York. "Coherent Light Emission from GaAs Junctions" was its title. The signers were R. N. Hall, G. E. Fenner, J. D. Kingsley, T. J. Soltys, and R. O. Carlson.

The *Applied Physics Letters* of the same date carried a short paper signed by five scientists of the Thomas J. Watson Research Center of the International Business Machines Corportion at Yorktown Heights, New York. "Stimulated Emission of Radiation from GaAs p-n Junctions" was its title. The signers were Marshall I. Nathan, William P. Dumke, Gerald Burns, Frederick H. Dill, Jr., and Gordon Lasher.

(Multi-man teams of this kind are common in advanced research today. Problems are complex, apparatus is elaborate and expensive, the areas of knowledge to be mastered are vast. Everywhere in laser research there is pressure and urgency. Priority in discovery is important, not only for honor, but because of patents and the profits involved.)

Who would have priority with the "injection laser"? When publication dates are identical, the custom is to award the "first" to the contender whose paper was first received by the journal printing it. On this basis the GE paper, received September 24, nosed out the IBM paper, received October 4.

So keen and close is competition in the laser race!

The third team which independently achieved injected laser operation was that of Keyes and Quist of Lincoln Laboratories, who had made the first breakthrough the previous July.

Scientists at IBM Research Center observe electronic characteristics of their new gallium arsenide direct injection laser. They are, from left to right, Gordon J. Lasher, William P. Dumke, Gerald Burns, Marshall I. Nathan and Frederick H. Dill, Jr.

No doubt remains today whether semiconductor diodes can be made to operate as lasers by means of injection methods. The question now is, rather, how far and how fast can the new method of operation be developed.

The announcements of the injection lasers were launched with press conferences, newspaper and magazine stories in the last months of 1962. The unusual circumstances of the race intensified interest in the device. That interest is not likely to wane soon, even though a vast amount of work remains to be done.

Portrait of an Injection Laser. The first injection lasers differed in details but were alike in all important essentials. Here we shall give a general picture, not a particular one (Figure 12.2).

We see what looks like a sandwich—a very tiny one. Actually it is a single crystal, *not* three separate pieces fitted together. In the n region the dominant impurity introduced during manufacture is a "donor" type of substance, such as tellurium. It "donates" or releases electrons to move through the crystal lattice.

In the p region, however, the dominant impurity is an "acceptor" type of substance, such as zinc. It "accepts" or hold fast to, electrons, thus creating holes, which act like positive charges as they move through the crystal lattice.

And between the two regions lies the all-important junction or transition zone. It is here that the radiation emerges.

This, we emphasize again, is a *tiny* sandwich. It is tiny essentially because laser action requires an extremely high density or concentration of current at the junction. The junction is made small to increase this concentration or electron crowding.

171

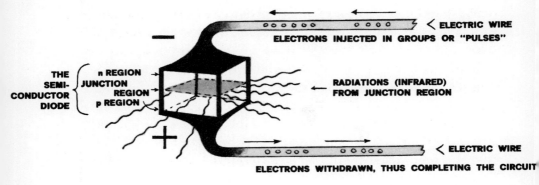

ELECTRIC WIRE
ELECTRONS INJECTED IN GROUPS OR "PULSES"

THE
SEMI-
CONDUCTOR
DIODE
{ n REGION
JUNCTION
REGION
p REGION

RADIATIONS (INFRARED)
FROM JUNCTION REGION

ELECTRIC WIRE
ELECTRONS WITHDRAWN, THUS COMPLETING THE CIRCUIT

Figure 12.2 Portrait (imaginary) of an injection laser in action.

Powerful, pulsed electric current injects hosts of electrons (moving negative charges) into the **n** region.

The circuit is completed by withdrawing electrons from the **p** region.

The energy jumps and the resulting radiations take place in the plane of the junction region, between the **n** and **p** regions.

The minus (−) and plus (+) are the usual electric signs. Remember that the electrons **enter** here where the sign is minus, and they **leave** here where the sign is plus.

The actual junction areas of the first injection lasers were in the range between about ⅛ and ⅟₁₀₀ of a square millimeter. This is very small. You can get some idea of how small by looking at 1 square centimeter and recalling that it contains 100 square millimeters!

Such injection lasers are kept intensely cold. They are immersed in liquid nitrogen or helium. Thus they tend to be brought to temperatures of about 80° K, nearly 200° C. below the freezing point of water.

The injected currents are very brief, but powerful. They are, in fact, pulses lasting somewhere between five and twenty-five *millionths* of a second. During this tiny instant the current

172

density becomes enormous. In the first G.E. diode lasers, the coherent emission accompanied "jolts" of current as large as twenty thousand amperes per square centimeter of crystal surface. The IBM diodes were driven by pulses ranging as high as 100 thousand amperes per square centimeter of junction area.

Photomicrograph of the new injection laser that is powered directly by an electrical current rather than an external light source. The dark rectangle at the center of the greatly enlarged picture is the actual injection laser which measures a mere 0.005 x 0.04 inches. Surrounding it is a flat metallic support which also serves as an electrical connection. The wire coming from the top is a second electrical connection.

Courtesy IBM CORPORATION

Had currents of such strength been maintained for even as long as $\frac{1}{100}$ second, the diodes would certainly have been distorted, perhaps even destroyed, by the heat which would have built up inside them. The melting point of gallium arsenide (GaAs) is 1,240° C. At concentrations of 20 to 100 thousand amperes per square centimeter, this temperature would soon be attained, were not the pulses quite brief.

It seems probable that future injection lasers will be "driven" by pulses, rather than by continuous currents, unless drastically different substances can be utilized for forming the diodes.

Ordinary irregular spontaneous radiation begins at relatively low electric-current levels. The IBM report shows, for example, that such radiation could be detected when the injected current averaged only one ampere per square centimeter of junction area. But real coherent laser radiation did not get well under way until that intensity was increased more than ten thousand times.

The start of laser action follows a typical pattern—a pattern observed in other types of lasers, and closely parallel to the pattern of the onset of masering in maser devices. As stimulated emission begins its chain reaction, there is (*i*) a sharp rise in power of emitted radiation, and (*ii*) a marked narrowing of the frequency range or band width in which this power is emitted.

In the laser stage the injection device shows a sharp rise in radiated energy. The great landslide of photon emission is under way. Photons stimulate emission of additional photons. The great flood of emission rises high over the absorptions. A frenzy of radiation seems to have come over the electrons moving through the junction region of the diode.

174

Before the laser level is reached, each increase in current strength brings a proportional increase in power of emitted radiation. But once the laser level is attained, each increase in current strength is accompanied by an ever higher rate of increase of radiation. Here, again, stimulated emission builds swiftly, like a chain reaction.

Tops in Efficiency. We have seen that other lasers converted only a small amount of their pumping power into coherent radiations. Injection lasers, on the other hand, show an amazing efficiency. It appears that almost all of the electrical energy injected into them is converted into the energy of emitted light.

Pumping of crystal lasers by means of powerful flash tubes has been called a "brute-force" method of exciting atoms. The flash tube drenches the crystal, not only with the photons its active atoms can absorb, but with frequencies that are wasted and many that serve only to overheat its structure.

The energizing of injection lasers by means of electric currents is quite different. The current consists, as always, of streams of electrons, identical negative charges. The structure of the crystal itself and the effects of the "doping" substances in the diode establish the size of the downward energy jumps by electrons at the junction zone. Each such jump means emission of a photon of corresponding size.

One may ask: Where is the population reversal in an injection laser?

It is there, of course, or there would be no laser action—but it is there in a form different from that in other lasers.

Injection lasers appear to offer one other advantage. They are the first truly controllable lasers. If we vary the strength of pulses fed into an injection laser, we should get a corresponding variation in the strength of the resulting radiation. This means that laser output can be directly modulated.

Modulation is the process which impresses messages—voice, music, pictures, and other information—on the carrier waves of radio and microwave radiation. Before the birth of injection lasers there seemed no suitable means for directly modulating laser radiation, even if it could be produced with sufficient power and purity to serve as a carrier wave.

A look at the future of lasers and masers. The future of injection lasers seems enormous. Even an imaginative writer of science fiction might hesitate to predict all the possibilities. Such devices and techniques have a way of opening new doors as they develop. Additional breakthroughs may come in the most unexpected directions.

This much seems certain: if the second, third, and following decades of maser-laser development maintain the tempo of the first, then this new family of devices will rank with the vacuum tube and the transistor as the great transformers of human life and human prospects.

Many newspaper and magazine stories have stressed the death-dealing possibilities of lasers. If they can already vaporize diamonds and burn away steel in the twinkling of an eye, they can be developed to shoot down missiles in flight or annihilate soldiers or civilians at a distance.

Lasers, like so many other advanced devices, can doubtless be developed to deal destruction and death. Let us stress, however, what they may do for the peaceful progress of mankind. A future in which men had to fear laser death rays ready to rain down on earth from orbiting satellites would be a future in which men themselves, as well as their amazing

176

masers and lasers, would be lost in a nightmare of annihilation.

Essence of the processes known as *masering* and *lasering*, we have seen, is the concerted, cooperative actions of atoms and molecules. They radiate powerfully because they radiate together. Coherent radiation results from united action by the individual emitters.

Men and nations may well learn from this remote example.

Masers and lasers, as we see, reach long roots into the rich past of science. They are to be understood in the light of knowledge that we owe to some of the greatest names in science:

Isaac Newton; Michael Faraday, that prince of experimenters who said, "Nothing is too wonderful to be true!"; James Clerk Maxwell; Albert Einstein, whose insights transformed modern science; and many other men of good will and humanity, as well as of superb scientific comprehension.

We may look toward the future in the hope that these latest and amazing examples of man's growing mastery over the forces of inanimate nature will be known not as sources of added human dread and despair, but as instruments which serve human communication, human welfare, and human life.

INDEX

179